RULES FOR NEW YORK SPORTS FANS

Joe Benigno
with Jordan Raanan

TRIUMPH
B O O K S

Triumph Books and colophon are registered trademarks of Random House, Inc.

Library of Congress Cataloging-in-Publication Data

Benigno, Joe.
  Rules for New York sports fans / Joe Benigno with Jordan Raanan.
     p. cm.
  ISBN 978-1-60078-309-8
  1. Sports—New York (State)—New York—Miscellanea. 2. Sports spectators—New York (State)—New York. I. Raanan, Jordan. II. Title.
  GV584.5.N4B46 2010
  796.09747'1—dc22
                                      2009040904

This book is available in quantity at special discounts for your group or organization. For further information, contact:

   Triumph Books
   542 South Dearborn Street
   Suite 750
   Chicago, Illinois 60605
   (312) 939-3330
   Fax (312) 663-3557
   www.triumphbooks.com

Printed in U.S.A.
ISBN: 978-1-60078-309-8

Design by Patricia Frey
All photos courtesy of Getty Images unless otherwise noted

To the greatest and most passionate sports fans in the world, New York sports fans.

CONTENTS

Part Four: Gearing Up

Part Five: Watch It

Part Six: In the House

Part Seven: Booing and Cheering

Part Eight: And Don't Forget

Part Nine: Calling All FANs

ACKNOWLEDGMENTS

Nothing would be possible without my wonderful wife, Terry, who has been there through it all.

To WFAN program director Mark Chernoff and the venerable Mike Francesa, this would not be possible without you. You helped get me to where I am today.

Thanks to Jordan for dealing with me throughout this process. We both know that is not easy.

Finally, an extra special thanks to all the fans, especially the ones who helped make this book happen. You have been there since the beginning.

—JB

Everything I do begins and ends with my wonderful wife, Abby. She is my rock, my heart and soul, always and forever. Her support and encouragement drives me to be a better person every day. The fact that she can deal with the most annoying person alive each and every day, especially while I was writing this book, gets her a permanent pass into my Hall of Fame.

My mom and dad are equally impressive, always there for me through good and bad to guide me in the right direction. For that, I am forever indebted. How did I get so lucky to have an entire family (in-laws included) ready to help at the drop of a hat? I hit the DNA jackpot.

Also, thanks to all my friends—particularly Bubbleball participants—for not killing me when I cluttered everyone's inboxes with incessant questions. The only one who dealt with more questions than my friends was Joe, who remained patient despite my constant pestering and welcomed me into his world in order to make this book happen. I feel fortunate to have worked with him on this project. Common sense says it would have never made it off the ground without him.

Finally, there is my omnipresent wife who, like I said before, bookends everything I've done since we've met. Lucky me.

—JR

From Both of Us
A special thanks to everyone at Triumph Books for being so supportive and patient. We know it's not easy to work with either of us individually, much less together.

Tom Bast shepherded this vague idea from its infantile stages and turned it into something real. That is a miracle unto itself. Adam Motin pushed us to get writing and helped fill any holes that existed. Katy Sprinkel took care of everything else. She necessarily edited, deleted, and changed 10 times over. All your hard work is greatly appreciated.

And a special thanks to our agent, Mark Lepselter, for taking care of the details and making the deal happen. It was great teamwork all the way around.

INTRODUCTION

BY JORDAN RAANAN

Inside stadiums, arenas, bars, homes, and offices across the Tri-State area, sports fans are subconsciously abiding by a set of unwritten rules. These are not the traditional bylaws that dictate everyday behavior, the "law of the land" that is enforced by police. The rules for New York sports fans are something different. They comprise a code that guides the actions, rituals, and routines of something seemingly natural: rooting for one's favorite team.

For most of you, these rules are so deeply ingrained that you don't even realize you're adhering to them. It's like swinging a bat—you just get up and do it, no questions asked. You've done it so many times before that it requires little effort or thought. On the other hand, if you take someone who has never played baseball or softball in his life and put a bat in his hand, the result might not be pretty. You'd be much more likely to get Jeff Gillooly than Albert Pujols.

But so many of you have rooted for your team since Day One that it's become like second nature. You cheer, boo, clap, and yell like you always have, and you do it without hesitation. You never read a book or researched on the Internet to figure out the required actions or the appropriate reactions. That's what makes being a fan so beautiful: it's so natural and unrehearsed. It's your true emotions being dictated by nothing other than the actions on the field.

Rooting for your favorite team is a passion so many New Yorkers share. You've done it since you were young, and it's something you will continue to do when you're old. Our goal in writing *Rules for New York Sports Fans* is just to make sure you, as New York sports fans, do it right. And most of the time you do. For many of you, it's an innate sensibility. You probably don't need much help, just a little refinement. That's where we come in.

There are some who violate these rules regularly, and more often than not they don't realize the errors of their ways. We're not blaming them either. They just don't know any better. It's because of this that our idea came to fruition in the first place. By putting the rules on paper, we can ensure that New York fans know right from wrong when it comes to being a real fan. And since nobody has come forth before now to show the way, who better to do it than us—two guys who are admittedly one-dimensional, die-hard New York sports fans?

We know sports. We live sports. It's a huge part of our lives, and it's no accident it's also a part of our jobs. It's our passion, hobby, and lifeline. It defines who we are. Without it, we are hollow—and we're not embarrassed to admit it either.

When you think about a true die-hard New York sports fan, someone who lives and dies with every game and move their team makes, whether it's good or bad, Joe Benigno is clearly your man. He's the epitome of a die-hard fan. He's the Adonis of sports fans. Once just Joe from Saddle River and a regular caller to WFAN, he's worked his way up to become a midday host in the nation's biggest market at the nation's most successful sports radio station. He's also a regular contributor at SNY, the television home of the New York Mets, one of Joe's favorite teams.

Through his years at WFAN, Joe has become one of the most well-liked and respected sports-media figures in New York—and that's saying a lot. After all, New York is filled with all kinds of sports icons. More often than not, the best of the best find their way to the big city.

It is no accident that Joe has become one of them. The true fans, the real fans, the die-hard fans, love him. The reason is simple: Joe is one of them. He's a realist, willing to tell it like it is, no matter the situation. He's passionate and knowledgeable beyond belief. He wants to see his teams win more than anything in the world. Unfortunately for Joe, he went wrong somewhere a long time ago during the selection process. It's been a rocky road since the '70s for Joe, a Mets, Jets, Rangers, and Knicks fan.

The lack of success doesn't matter one bit. Joe will never ditch his teams, just as he hasn't changed since becoming a successful sports radio and television personality. Most important—and this is why everyone loves him—Joe is still just a fan.

Joe received a break when he guest-hosted a show in 1994. The great Eddie Coleman was also in the room, but Joe didn't need him. He didn't need anyone or anything except his passion. That alone was enough for listeners to realize that he was special.

That show was enough on its own to catapult Joe into the business. The rants that made him famous as a caller soon made him famous as a host. Soon enough, he was hosting the overnights and then the midday show at WFAN. His following kept growing. The people had spoken. They loved having this die-hard Jets, Mets, Knicks, and Rangers fan as their on-air representative. Superfan Joe had made it big, opening his shows with classic rants that became can't-miss radio, especially on those Monday mornings following the latest Jets collapse.

"Oh, the pain," Joe bellowed about his Jets, Mets, Knicks, or Rangers in the opening segment of a show. With those three words, Joe had listeners hooked. He had the natural ability to describe exactly what his listeners were thinking and feeling. "What a disaster. What a disaster," he would say later. It was another patented three-word Joe-ism that summed up the situation perfectly. You couldn't say it better yourself, and you didn't need to. Joe was there for you. The fan's fan had made it big.

Joe made it because he had principles. He followed the unwritten rules for New York sports fans. He has never put on a jersey from another team or rooted for a rival. He almost never misses a Jets or Mets game, and he wouldn't even think of missing a playoff game. Joe sets forth in the following pages all the rules New York sports fans should know intuitively. They are rules that have subconsciously guided his decisions and actions for years, and which have become the foundation for his professional success. They helped him get to where he is today. They are what make him the quintessential New York sports fan.

No matter what he's achieved, he is still just Joe from Saddle River—well, now it's Joe from Old Tappan, but it's the same difference. He's the same guy, the same fan of the same teams. He still possesses the same voracious desire to see his teams win. Joe is a fan who happens to work in the media. That's what made it so natural to look in his direction when this project starting coming to light. That's always who I've strived to be: a Joe Benigno, someone whose passion is evident.

The idea to write this book crossed my mind many years back. I would find myself at games, bars, hanging with friends, or just walking around, and I saw behavior that absolutely shocked me. I couldn't believe the naïvete and blatant disregard that certain people showed for something I held in such high regard: fandom. How could someone say they rooted for the Giants *and* the Jets? Were they crazy? How could someone root for their fantasy player against their favorite team? Who could say that they used to root for the Knicks but don't anymore?

These people had no idea they offended me. But I felt embarrassed to be with them, ashamed to know them, and infuriated by their cluelessness. I didn't want to be in the same room as them a second longer than I had to. They desecrated something I consider one of the most important things in life: loyalty.

Hopefully, with this book, it will never happen again. The rules set out in these chapters can help those flagrant fans correct their errors. After all, there is always room for self-improvement, even among the best of us. As we wrote this book, I discovered a few rules that I was breaking along the way. I considered myself the perfect model of a New York sports fan, yet I was letting work get in the way of fandom. I was letting my job as a sports reporter in Philadelphia dilute the passion I felt for my New York teams. Don't get me wrong, I'll never ditch my teams and start rooting for Philadelphia's clubs. I've never considered it, and I never will. I get the question all the time: "Are you a Philly fan yet?" To me, it doesn't even make sense. It's not in my biological makeup. How could I turn my back on such a large part of my childhood and my identity as an adult? It's not going to happen.

Yet I was becoming everything I had always preached I wouldn't become. I was a media member first and a fan second. I needed to remember why I started in this business in the first place: because there was nothing I liked to do more than watch or play sports. Since my physical talents weren't quite on par with those at a professional level, I went the other route: I was going to cover sports.

Somewhere along the way, though, I stopped enjoying the games. Writing this book has given me a chance to step back and realize that I don't want to have my Real Sports Fan card confiscated. I needed to practice what I preached. I needed to see *Rules for New York Sports Fans* in print as much as anyone else.

I am proud to say that I've rejoined Joe as a true, die-hard New York sports fan. It's a very large and distinguished group that we're both very proud to be a part of. Nowhere else are there more passionate, knowledgeable fans so deeply committed to winning. That's exactly what we love. That's exactly what New York sports fans are and what we're proud to be.

Of course, any New York sports fan knows when we talk about New York teams, we're including any team whose home base is in New Jersey, Connecticut, or the five boroughs of New York City. That list includes Major League Soccer's Red Bulls (who have the New York name but play in New Jersey) and the NFL's Giants and Jets, themselves based across the Hudson. The name and home state don't matter—as Tri-State fans, we hold together. Same goes for golf, as well as tennis...really, for any sport, large or small.

For the sake of brevity, in this book we tackle the four sports that command the most attention in the New York metropolitan area: baseball, football, basketball, and hockey. We avoid college sports for the most part too, since there aren't many college sports teams in the Tri-State area that have a wide-ranging fan base consisting in large part of nongraduates. In New York, the professional teams rule—so too do they in our book.

That said, we're going to stick with what we know and are. As golfer Phil Mickelson said before the 2009 U.S. Open, "I love the New York sports fans because they get it." Joe definitely gets it. I think I get it. Let's hope this helps you get it too. After all, all we want is for each of us to be the best fan we can be.

PART ONE

THE ONE AND ONLY

RULE #1

THE GOLDEN RULE: ONLY ONE TEAM PER SPORT

We've all heard it before: "I root for both the Mets and the Yankees." Many a so-called fan has prefaced a sports commentary in this way. But right there with that simple, telling phrase, the conversation is ostensibly over. What inevitably follows is a qualifier or attempted justification of joint loyalty, but it doesn't really matter. You've already tuned them out. Their credibility is already shot as a die-hard fan for either team.

There is no such thing as a Mets *and* Yankees fan in New York. Just as there should be no Cubs *and* White Sox fan in Chicago or no Dodgers *and* Angels fan in Southern California. No one who calls himself a real fan can root for both teams without declaring one the clear favorite. Maybe in other parts of the country it flies to root for more than one team, but in New York it's not kosher. It's the number one rule for any sports fan: there is only one favorite team allowed per sport. No exceptions.

Therefore, it's either the Mets or Yankees; Giants or Jets; Rangers, Islanders, or Devils; Knicks or Nets. You must stick with your team until death do you part. Or until they pull a Dodgers- or Giants-style relocation for the fine wine and weather in California.

PEDRO MARTINEZ
Who's his daddy?

There are no divorces allowed citing irrevocable differences. And you certainly don't cheat or keep another team on the side. Maybe you flirt with a team during a playoff run or something, but you never embrace a new long-term partner.

Having two favorite teams in the same sport is like saying you support communism and democracy. It's like having no preference between chocolate and vanilla or being a fan of both the Grateful Dead and the Pussycat Dolls. It just doesn't make any sense to have both.

Aside from the ethical conflict, the practical explanations as to why it's truly impossible to be a real fan of two teams in the same sport are threefold.

Emotional attachment is the barometer for a person's level of fandom. True fans, die-hard fans, fully commit themselves to the successes and failures of their team. It's actually eerily similar to being in a relationship. You're either in or you're out. You're either in love or you're not. You live and die with every pitch, quarter, or period, or you care so little that you're willing to cheat on them with a better option.

The casual fan is very similar to the serial dater. They pop in and out of love, testing the waters. Their loyalty is strong—until it isn't. How can someone call himself a fan of any team when he roots for Roger Clemens and Mike Piazza? It's equivalent to dating Beyonce one day and Rosie O'Donnell the next. It's just confounding. You can't have it both ways. You either wanted to take that splintered bat and shove it into Clemens' heartless chest or you begged to see Piazza stop whining and continue on with the game. It was one or the other; there was no middle ground. This is usually the case with allegiances to New York sports teams: there is a line in the sand that's impossible to straddle.

That line definitely exists with the Mets and Yankees, even more so than the other local combinations (see: The Most Egregious New York Combos). Like Piazza and Clemens, the Yankees and Mets are like oil and water. The Yankees are the rich big brother with a long history of success—27 world championships, to be exact—while the Mets are the struggling, unemployed, younger sibling who came along much later (1962, when the Yankees already had 19 titles under their belt). The Mets have experienced much more heartbreak and many more turbulent times. They have two hard-won World Series titles and a dubious history of underachievement. Even their talent-rich teams of the late-'80s, which included two superstars seemingly destined for Hall of Fame status in Dwight Gooden and Darryl Strawberry, didn't completely live up to expectations. They won just one championship and two division titles with those two players—and neither Gooden nor Strawberry's jerseys are retired by the team. As Sonny from *A Bronx Tale* said, "The saddest thing in life is wasted talent."

If Doc and Darryl's disappointments with the Mets don't exemplify how badly things went wrong, this statistic might: the two players won more championships in their seven combined years with the Yankees—when both players were in their thirties— than they did in 19 quality years with the Mets. Gooden even threw a no-hitter for the Yankees. Those facts don't sit well with any Mets fan, and they shouldn't.

Die-hard fans couldn't possibly have true emotional attachment to both teams simultaneously, no matter how much they like an individual player. It's part of the biological makeup of a real New York fan. Rooting for both would be sensory overload. What would happen when the twice-yearly Subway Series rolls around? Do you root for a tie? What happens when David Wright steps to the plate against Mariano Rivera? Do you root for a walk? Or want an intentional walk ordered? Then consider the ultimate dilemma: Which side did you take when the Mets and Yankees met in the 2000 World Series? Did you declare it a win-win situation?

Fans always have favorites. That's just what they are programmed to do. That's what makes them fans. Phony fans hedge their bets and root for both teams, which is just another way of saying they support whoever wins.

Fundamentally, simultaneously rooting for two teams equally is impossible, *especially* if those two teams are playing against one another. You can't root for a strikeout and a walk, a goal and a save, a touchdown and an interception, or a steal and a basket at the same time. It's impractical and illogical. There has to be a prohibitive favorite one way or the other.

If you pick a team depending on who is better that year, you're a *frontrunner*. If you pick depending on who needs the victory more, you're a *situational fan*. If you pick depending on your mood that day, you're a *fair-weather fan*. If you just pick whoever is winning, you're a *bandwagon jumper*. None of these are labels that any true fan who has invested time, energy, and money into rooting for any of the teams with all their might would wear. Part of being a fan is experiencing the ups and downs that come with each season, bringing us to the second reason a real New York sports fan can only have one favorite team per sport.

No Pain, No Gain
Unfortunately, pain is a necessary evil in the experience of being a fan, no matter what team you support. Of course, the success of a team, and thus the amount of pain endured, can vary greatly. Regardless, painful defeats are inevitable. It's a hazard that comes when you sign on the dotted line and place your emotions in the hands of your chosen franchise. There is no way around it for a real fan—especially a committed, loyal New York sports fan who completely invests his emotions. And besides, how much fun would it be if your team won every single year?

My Red Sox Flirtation

As a Mets fan, I wouldn't root for another team—and especially not the Yankees. **Never** the Yankees. But there was one time when I felt a lot of pain for a team that wasn't my own. It was the same pain I would have felt had it happened to the Mets.

It was the 2003 Red Sox-Yankees series, when Aaron Boone hit the home run off Tim Wakefield to win it. I was rooting for the Red Sox in that one. I always liked them, even from the early days. Perhaps it had something to do with the fact that they were the Yankees' archrival. I won't go so far as to say the Red Sox are my secondary team, but I have always liked them since I was a little kid. It goes back to my father and another Italian guy from Boston, Tony Conigliaro.

I don't have an emotional attachment to the Red Sox, but that one game, Game 7 of the 2003 ALCS, really got to me. I think it was because it was the Yankees and they'd beaten the Red Sox so many times. To me, it's the most one-sided rivalry in sports.

And boy, did I kill Pedro Martinez that night on the air. I didn't kill Grady Little for not taking him out. It was all Pedro—and that was supposed to be his signature moment. I was doing the overnight and I watched the game with my producer at the time, Ray Martel. "Sugar Ray" is from Providence, Rhode Island, and not surprisingly, he's a Red Sox fan. We watched the game in the conference room at the FAN. The game ended I don't know what time, maybe 12:15 AM or so, and we were scheduled to go on the air at 1:00 AM. I looked at Ray and said, "How the hell are we going to do the show? How are we going to do the show?"

That was the only time I felt a real emotional attachment to another team. I felt terrible! It was a combination of wanting to see the Yankees finally lose to the Red Sox and the fact that the Sox hadn't won for, at that point, 85 years. Every time they played the Yankees in a big situation they lost, whether it was the Bucky Dent game, the playoffs in '99, or any number of other games. All of the pennant races in the '40s and '50s, losing the last game of the season to the Yankees in 1949 and 1978, the fact that the Red Sox had never won a World Series—it all percolated in me that night. I've rooted for the Red Sox in every World Series they've played in during my lifetime (with exception to 1986 against the Mets, of course). In 1967, when the Red Sox played the Cardinals, I was rooting for them. In 1975 against Cincinnati, I was definitely rooting for them.

In 1986, there was no question that I rooted for the Mets. I thank the Red Sox for giving us the World Series. If it wasn't for them, we wouldn't have one. I wasn't paying attention that year when they beat the Angels in that amazing series in the ALCS. I was too wrapped up in my team. For me, the Mets are my one and only. But I do like the Red Sox, I'll admit it. —JB

Even the Yankees, the most successful team in professional sports, have experienced plenty of heartbreaking moments. In 1996, when they won their first World Series in 18 years, their fans remembered Edgar Martinez's double down the line bringing home Ken Griffey Jr., which helped the Mariners clinch the 1995 ALDS. The demoralizing loss made the '96 moment that much more enjoyable when Charlie Hayes squeezed Mark Lemke's foul pop for the final out. Even seeing former Red Sox star Wade Boggs ride around the outfield on a horse didn't temper the enthusiasm.

The feeling of ultimate achievement wouldn't be the same if you supplanted your team's failure or loss with the success of another team. You can't be on the Mets' bandwagon only when the Yankees struggle. If that were the case, there would be no real joy in seeing the Yankees defeat the Mets in six games in the Subway Series and seeing Piazza's fly ball off Mariano Rivera fall short and land in the glove of Bernie Williams.

Rooting for both teams is cheating on your emotions. As someone who roots for both teams, you didn't feel the pain of a true Mets fan because you were busy enjoying the spoils of a Yankees victory. But you also weren't experiencing the same joy as a true Yankees fan, that extra sense of accomplishment that comes from besting a rival.

If everyone were fans of both teams, then rivalry wouldn't exist at all. At last check, you can't argue, bicker, or gloat with yourself. If you do, we recommend consulting a doctor immediately.

Time Is of the Essence

As if cheating on your emotions isn't enough, there is also the literal impossibility of rooting for more than one team at the same time. There just aren't enough minutes in a season for a fan to invest in more than one team from the same sport.

Being a real fan is a time-consuming proposition (see Rule #15) when done right. This is especially true in baseball. With 162 games in the season and mostly overlapping start times for the Mets and Yankees, following both contests on a nightly basis is impossible. Added to which, the baseball season—spanning March to September, and into October and now November if you include the postseason—overlaps every other major professional sport's season. It's unrealistic for anyone, no matter how enthusiastic, to put that kind of time investment into two teams in the same sport. One team is more than enough.

things
JETS FANS
love

J-E-T-S CHANT
J-E-T-S! Jets! Jets! Jets!
It has a nice ring to it.

That's why the Golden Rule of real New York sports fans is the fundamental, essential concept. It just makes sense. Case closed, no exceptions. Say it with me: *I will not root for the Mets and the Yankees; the Giants and the Jets; the Knicks and Nets; or the Rangers, Islanders, and Devils. I will devote my attention to my one and only team.*

And don't go embracing teams outside the Tri-State area either. You simply can't have the necessary emotional attachment, experience the appropriate amount of pain (you know what they say: no pain, no gain), or invest the proper time into two teams. Not on the East Coast and certainly not with New York's amazing, loyal, and knowledgeable fan bases.

The Most Egregious New York Combos

Rooting for two or more teams in the same sport is bad no matter who they are. Still, some are worse than others—particularly crosstown rivals. But no pairing is more egregious than the Mets and the Yankees.

Mets-Yankees

They're not in the same league. They only play each other six times each season. They've clashed just once in the playoffs, in the 2000 World Series. And yet, they're still somehow bitter enemies. Calling them "co-favorites" would undoubtedly be uncivilized.

The reason is simple: it's all about jealousy. Mets fans are envious of the Yankees' success and seemingly endless resources. They can't stand to see the latest CC Sabathia, A.J. Burnett, or Mark Teixeira join the "Evil Empire"—and they most certainly can't stomach watching another champagne-pouring orgy on the other side of town while their team chokes down the stretch. Again. Oh, the pain.

Yankees fans, meanwhile, would rather underachieve in peace than hear criticism from Mets fans—not to mention everyone else around the country—each time they fall short of winning the World Series. No matter how big, bad, and mighty the Yankees are, there have been many more seasons that ended with heartbreak rather than trophy hoisting. Mets fans are always there when the seasons end in disappointment to kindly provide a reminder.

BROOKLYN

Will it ever come to fruition?

The Yankees are the baseball equivalent to Apple. They put out a top-notch product, make the most money, spend it on their players, carry an elitist attitude, and have a constant expectation to win. The Mets are Dell. They have plenty of resources at their disposal, try to be the more efficient organization, and are always attempting, mostly unsuccessfully, to jump ahead of the behemoth. They always seem to be the up-and-coming team trying to compete and become the big,

My Near Miss

I'll admit it: I rooted for the Mets when they won the World Series in 1986. (This is not a violation. See Rule 2) I was seven years old and don't remember much about that season or the now-classic Series against the Red Sox. But I do recall asking my brother, the black sheep of our family as a Mets fan, to wake me up for the ninth inning of Game 7. He tried, but couldn't do it. I was dead asleep.

I guess it was a sign from above. I don't ever remember pulling for the Mets after that season. Not in '88 when they were dominated by Orel Hersheiser in the playoffs or in '89 and '90 when they were still one of baseball's best teams.

The 1986 series happened before my allegiance to the Yankees was solidified. At that age, I didn't know any better. I must not have realized my entire family—with the exception of my brother, of course—was composed of Yankees fans.

It was long before I declared myself. I was too young to have my Mets fan friends calling me to throw salt in the wounds after every tough Yankees loss and each Mets triumph. There was no Subway Series or Roger Clemens-Mike Piazza line-in-the-sand moment to consider. There were no college roommates using Mariano Rivera's picture as a dartboard target. All of that would come later and help shape me into the die-hard Yankees fan I am today. But for that brief moment in '86, I won't deny it: I was rooting for the Mets. Don't worry, there's no chance of that ever happening again. Rules are rules. —JR

bad bully. In the meantime, the bully knocks them down repeatedly. How can you possibly root for the bully and his favorite target at the same time?

When the Mets were born in 1962, they built much of their fan base from those people who were fundamentally opposed to the Yankees' flash. Many of them had been proponents of the Brooklyn Dodgers. Manager Casey Stengel, summarily dismissed from the Yankees as "too old," took the helm for the fledgling Mets. They became the "Lovable Losers" that their fans have taken up for. The underdog to the Yankees' top dog.

This is exactly what makes it so taboo to be a fan of both. And since baseball is the most popular sport in New York, it's worse to call yourself a Mets and a Yankees fan than any other local same-sport combo, even if they don't cross each other's paths very often in the course of a season. The two sides have never mixed well or liked each other much. For real Mets and Yankees fans, that will never change.

Rangers-Islanders-Devils
Any two out of these three is bad since they all play in the Eastern Conference's Atlantic Division and meet each other six times per season. Three out of three isn't even on the table— that's beyond embarrassing. If that's the case, why stop there? You might as well just root for every team in the NHL. With the local trifecta alone, you come close to guaranteeing yourself a win every single night during the regular season.

And let's not forget, the Rangers, Islanders, and Devils have met countless times in the playoffs. The Jets and Giants, never. The Knicks and Nets, just a handful of times. Even the Mets and Yankees have met just once. Hockey is different. Eight teams in each conference go to the postseason. That's left a long list of playoff matchups—most incredibly intense—between the teams. With three teams out of 15 in the Eastern divison based in New York, the chances of more than one of them heading to the playoffs is a near certainty.

The rivalry between the Islanders and Rangers was stoked in the early '80s, when the Islanders beat the Rangers in four straight years en route to four Stanley Cup Final appearances and three titles. The Rangers clobbered both the Devils and the Islanders on their path to the Stanley Cup in 1994. In fact, the Hudson River Rivalry, played between the Rangers and Devils, has been ignited by five postseason meetings in the span between

FAN TIP

Go ahead and root for another nonrival team when your team is not playing.
Just don't develop a true emotional attachment.

1992 and 2009. The Rangers are also viewed as hockey's "Yankees" because of their endless resources and pompous attitude, just minus the championships.

Rooting for all three in the regular season is tough, but in the playoffs it becomes unfeasible. Fully investing your emotions into both the Devils and Rangers during their simultaneous 2009 NHL playoff runs would have required you to be in two places at one time. The two teams played a Game 7 in the first round at same time. How could you not watch a Game 7 live and from beginning to end? Picture in picture? Untenable! This alone should preclude you from rooting for more than one of the local hockey teams.

things
GIANTS FANS
love

DAVID TYREE'S HELMET
It "caught" the miracle Eli Manning pass in Super Bowl XLII. It is, quite simply, the greatest catch in NFL history.

Giants-Jets

Like the Mets and Yankees, they play in different leagues and rarely meet each other on the field. Also like the Mets and the Yankees, one team has a long and storied history of success. The Giants have been a top-notch franchise for three straight decades and boast three Super Bowl championships as a result. The Jets have been an embarrassment for much of their existence, with rare glimmers of success.

Similar to the crosstown baseball rivalry, Jets fans are envious of what the Giants have accomplished. Giants fans just laugh at the Jets' incompetence. It's a pretty combustible combination, but doesn't create anywhere near the level or resentment or animosity as the Mets and Yankees, for several reasons.

First, the NFL is a different beast. The Giants aren't the Yankees. Despite measurable success, they haven't dominated the league—or the back page. Additionally, because of beneficial network programming, the Giants and Jets never play at the same time, so it's possible to watch every one of both teams' games. In fact, many New York sports fans do.

The Giants and Jets play each other about once every four years—much less frequently than the Mets and Yankees and the local NHL teams. So while it wouldn't be advisable to be a Giants and a Jets fan, it's at least a bit more practical. Plus, with only 16 games in a season, it's less of a time investment. Which is to say, it's not the most despicable of propositions.

things NETS FANS hate

THE KNICKS

If they have a rival, it's their pompous and arrogant neighbors across the river.

Knicks-Nets

They're last on this list because they really haven't been good at the same time very often. When the Knicks were annual bridesmaids to Michael Jordan's Bulls' bride in the late '80s and into the '90s, the Nets were in the doldrums. In fact, nobody even really noticed the Nets were around during most of that time, with the exception of the Drazen Petrovic years. Even then, they were nowhere near serious contenders.

When the Nets finally came on at the beginning of the 21st century, with Jason Kidd starring, coach Isiah Thomas and president James Dolan's incompetence weighed down the Knicks. They were the punchline for a slew of jokes and the laughingstock of the league. The Nets pounded them consistently.

Sure, they meet more than a few times each season, but there isn't an established rivalry between them, despite the fact that the two teams are separated by less than eight miles. They have only met three times in the playoffs—all in the first round—and none of those series have been very competitive.

As a result, the rivalry and hatred between these two franchises has never really crystallized. Almost all the hatred comes from New Jersey, and that probably has a lot more to do with the way New Jersey natives view New Yorkers in general. Suffice it to say, there's not a lot of love lost. Still, this lack of a true, two-way rivalry makes it a bit easier to root for both teams than in any of the remaining major sports. Still, don't get us wrong—it's not recommended or respected.

PART TWO

SELECTION TIME

There comes a time when a decision has to be made and a team chosen. As Rule # 1 states, you can't waffle back and forth or possess a dual allegiance forever. As a matter of fact, we recommend being resolute from the start. Maybe it's all right to cheer for more than one team when you're in preschool or grade school and you don't know any better. But eventually a decision must be made—it's either one team or none. After all, it's already been made clear that there is no such thing as a real fan with two favorite teams in the same sport.

Picking a team might not be a life-or-death decision, but it is an important one. It's practically on par with selecting a spouse, and your team often lasts longer. For a die-hard fan, it might as well be a second marriage. Or, for the really sick ones out there, the team is the only love.

The decision to choose a favorite team should not be trifled with or taken lightly, especially since it is a choice that sticks forever (or should). Once a pick is made, just like the draft, there is no turning back. Take serious consideration in the team you choose, for it has serious consequences for your future. Your choice could result in a lifetime of frustration (we're talking to you, Jets fans) or happiness (that's right, Giants and Yankees fans). This one choice can make your winters miserable or content, your falls envious or fulfilled, your springs energized or lethargic.

Your decision is determined by a confluence of factors—some controllable and others nothing more than a combination of timing and circumstance. It can hinge on the influence of friends or family, geography, a specific player, the team's success at a certain moment in history, or even something as immaterial as your Little League team name or uniform color.

In New York, there seemed to be a fair amount of Charlotte Hornets fans upon their inception in the late '80s. Everybody loved the teal and the Larry Johnson "Grandmama" commercials. For kids growing up in the 1980s, they were an appealing choice. Especially as the Knicks faltered. The Oakland Raiders also have a similar appeal in the New York metropolitan area. The team simply has a mystique about them. Their reputation as "bad boys" is appealing to a certain type. Especially considering the smashmouth nature of football—these guys are just nasty and intimidating. And somehow, for some inexplicable reason, especially for Jets fans, there are way too many Dolphins fans in the area who love the aqua and orange. I blame Dan Marino, whose popularity as a quarterback elevated his team to lovable underdog status. Then there is America's team: the Dallas Cowboys. No doubt Yankees fans can relate to the Cowboys, who have more than their fair share of followers in the city. Of any team in the NFL, this one carries the tradition of excellence and the expectation for victory that Yankees put on the field every day.

Whatever guides an individual's choice to select a team isn't all that important, so long as it's well considered. There is only one major guideline for a New York sports fan to bear in mind when picking a favorite team.

RULE #2

SELECT A TEAM BY AGE 13

And the decision is a *final* decision. There are no backsies. The choice should not, barring extenuating circumstances, ever change. It doesn't matter if the team suddenly tanks or if an incompetent owner like James Dolan runs them (i.e., the New York Knicks). It doesn't matter if they sign or trade for your least favorite player (i.e., Roger Clemens and the Yankees) or hire an inadequate coach (i.e., the Jets' Joe Walton and Rich Kotite and the Giants' Bill Arnsparger and Ray Perkins). Part of being a fan is weathering the rough times. These are just speed bumps along the way, and a true fan needs to deal with them. Once you make that decision, you're hitched to the same train forever.

things
METS FANS
hate

CARDINALS AND CUBS
The Cardinals and the Mets went at it in the 1980 NLCS and again in 2006. Oh, the pain. The Cubs-Mets rivalry dates back to the late 1960s.

Then again, there are always loopholes. Say, for instance, that you never had a team. Of course you can adopt one later in life. This loophole applies *only* to individuals who never had an allegiance or had an acceptable reason for divorce.

Consider this example: you were born and raised in Nebraska. Since Nebraska doesn't have a local—or even remotely local—NBA team, professional basketball wasn't really on your radar. Then you moved to New York and started regularly attending Knicks games at Madison Square Garden. It's perfectly kosher for you to become a bona fide Knicks fan.

Now, if someone rooted for the Boston Celtics and moved to New York later in life, adopting the Knicks would be an unforgivable violation. A geographical move simply isn't grounds for divorce. You don't ditch your team when you move; your team lives *in you*. As such, once you reach the age of 13, you must show loyalty and stick with that team forever.

17

Why 13?

Thirteen is around the age when children begin to mature into young adults. They have either experienced puberty, are in the process, or will enter that pivotal stage soon. In essence, at 13 years old you are becoming a responsible adult, capable of making decisions and deciphering right and wrong as well as good and evil. Determining your team should be the first adult decision a person makes.

At 13, you will remember the significant moments that occur for the rest of you also r life. Part of the joy of being a sports fan is enjoying and remembering them, whether good or bad. At 13 years old, these are pictures that will be permanently plastered in the memory bank. It's well past the point of an individual's first memory, of course, but if your team wins a championship, a classic game, or an important series, it is a memory that will linger forever.

Prior to this, most sports fans are often in the discovery stage. They are still searching for the team that fits them best. Below are some of the most crucial factors young sports fans need to consider before finalizing their decision.

The Deciding Factors

Family

Choosing your team can go several different ways. The first and most common route for New York fans is to follow in their family's footsteps and root for the same team. This has the advantage of making each game and each season a true family bonding experience. You go to games together, spend holidays gathered around the TV. Conversation about the last play or the latest trade provides a constant conversation piece.

When you think about it, it just makes the most sense to go with the flow. That way, you eliminate the opportunity for contentious car rides and heated dinner table conversations. This is especially true when you're young, since you're almost always with your family. And if you're going to spend a lot of time

Some Knicks fans are born that way.

with your family, you might as well root with them, not against them.

It doesn't really matter who introduces you to the team either. It could be your father, mother, grandparent, cousin, or your crazy uncle. Either way, it's all the same. The bottom line is that family members often have a lot of influence, and deservedly so. You often admire them and spend a lot of time together during your most formative years.

Sometimes people don't have a choice in selecting a team. There are some parents who jam an allegiance down their children's throats right at birth. You know the type—the people who bring their kids home from the hospital wearing the Jets onesie and a baby bonnet version of the football helmet. For these kids, the choice can be practically unavoidable. We believe in allowing kids to make their own decisions. But convincing your children to be fans of the same team you root for isn't the worst thing in the world. It comes with plenty of benefits.

For many fathers and sons in particular, it can form a strong foundation for their relationship. Sports can be a common topic of conversation and one of the easiest and most convenient ways to bond. For many, including the two of us, it produces some of the most unforgettable childhood memories. That first time you attend a game with your dad is often something many boys never forget. That unbelievable play, that amazing game you witnessed together is an indelible memory. They are invaluable bonding experiences that wouldn't have happened without your shared devotion to the team.

Not everyone sides with their father or family. That's why there is a second avenue for the truly independent-minded sports fans who select a team in spite of their family. Some do it to be contrary—to irk their father, mother, or someone else. Others do it because they think it's funny, or because they want to distinguish themselves from everyone else. It happens. But the majority of New York fans still stick with the family tradition. The reason is simple: it's the easiest, most convenient, natural choice. Plus, you usually don't want to disappoint or disrespect your elders. Why rock the boat?

Geographic Location
Around the rest of the country and the world, this is probably the most common factor in adopting a team—it just flat-out makes sense to root for the home team. It's easy, convenient, and socially acceptable. You can attend games, show civic pride, and share the highs and lows with most of the people surrounding you. If you swim against the tide, don't expect too many invitations to parties, tailgates, or games. You could even be picked on at school or be ostracized, all because you picked Peyton Manning over Eli.

Choosing the local team also makes fiscal sense. It's a heck of a lot more convenient and less expensive to attend games nearby. Your parents will be grateful too. Come your birthday or Christmas, it will be much easier for them to find and purchase merchandise or tickets.

My Maiden Memory

That first sports-related memory seems to be incredibly random, and doesn't need to have anything to do with your favorite teams. Such is the case with my first sports memory.

It was the classic 1960 World Series between the Yankees and Pirates, when Bill Mazeroski hit a walk-off homer in Game 7. My father, a Yankees fan himself, promised me the hat of the winning team. The Mets franchise wouldn't be created for another two years. As a seven year old living in New York, I wanted that Yankees hat. I wanted the Yankees to win. I don't remember, but I'm sure I watched their games with my father.

Back then, the games were played during the day. We didn't listen to the game on the radio at school, so I didn't find out until after it was already over. Of course, bum luck, the Pirates won the World Series. I came home on the bus from school—I must have been in second grade—and found out that the Pirates had won. So my father came home with a Pirates hat—a hat that I definitely didn't want at all.

It wasn't my first experience with sports, but it's my first memory: the disappointment. Little did I know it was a sign of things to come. Boy, was I disappointed when I got off the bus after school and learned about Maz's now-legendary homer. It's something I will never forget. —JB

"...Blowing Your Mind Like You Knew We Would..."

I was six years old, just one month shy of my seventh birthday, in my first sports memory. It was January 1986, and the Chicago Bears routed the New England Patriots in Super Bowl XX. But let's back up a bit. My first sports memory was not from the day of the big game. It was from the week leading up to the contest. It was the Bears' "Super Bowl Shuffle" that caught my attention. And how could it not? Those rhymes were catchy. Ask any sports fan from my generation, and I bet you they can bust some "rhymes" from "The Super Bowl Shuffle." —JR

In the New York area it's a bit more complicated because the "home team" isn't the only home team. If you live in Kansas City, your choices are clear: the Royals for baseball and Chiefs for football. But in New York, there is more than one local team in every sport. So each fledgling sports fan stares down a tough decision: Yankees or Mets in baseball? Giants or Jets in football? Knicks or Nets in basketball? Rangers, Islanders, or Devils in hockey? Geography can only take you so far; it can't be the only

FAN TIP

Stay local. Don't root for a team located in a different region of the country.

factor in determining your allegiance. But it's still an important part of the process. The teams' players or their success during your formative years may prove as vital as the way that your family leans.

Of course, there are some New Yorkers who would tell you that the choice can be made across even stricter geographical lines. If you live in Queens, for instance, you're entrenched in Mets territory. If you're in the Bronx, Yankee Stadium's backyard, you'd be harder pressed to don the blue and orange. The Giants and the Jets might share a stadium, but look out into living rooms in Staten Island or Long Island, and we'd be willing to wager that you'll find more green and white than red and blue. Sure, party lines can be crossed, but local geography does come into play.

When conducting that initial search for a team to support, it's a good idea to start looking in your own neighborhood. It's just the right thing to do.

Players
Being attracted to a team because of a specific player is another determining factor. Newfangled terms such as "man crush" and "bromance" have put labels on a phenomenon that's been happening since the beginning of sports. Before Jeter and Wright there was the Babe, the Mick, the Duke, Joltin' Joe, Earl the Pearl, and Koufax. It's a simple concept: the stars bring fans to the stands.

In the 1960s, the Jets drafted a brash young quarterback who was as flashy on the field as he was off it. Soon enough, "Broadway" Joe Namath was driving crowds to the stadium and cementing a generation of football fans' allegiance to the New York Jets. Tom Seaver, a shut-down pitcher if ever there was one, did the same thing for the Mets in their early days. These stars were both instrumental in building their franchises' fan bases.

SELECTION TIME

Star power can be so great that it can eclipse all other factors in choosing a team. Dan Marino had fans flocking to the Dolphins in droves during the '80s. Michael Jordan had fans from all over the world clamoring for the Bulls in the '90s. It's perfectly fine—and understandable. Choosing a team based on the dominance of its star player is far from against the rules. But bear in mind that if you became a Bulls fan because of Jordan or a Dolphins fan because of Marino, those are your teams—for life. Don't come running to the Knicks, Nets, Jets, or Giants when your favorite player retires. Remember, there is no jumping on or off bandwagons after your 13th birthday.

Over the long run, you root for the uniform, not the player. College fans understand this. They see their team turn over every year in assembly-line fashion. It's just how the system works. While professional sports run differently, the underlying concept remains the same: It's the jersey that's most important. You don't abandon the franchise once your favorite player retires or gets traded or signs a huge contract with another team. A real fan hangs around during the lean years following a star's departure. It is a major violation of Rule #4 for a so-called fan to

Jet Set

I got hooked on my football team, the Jets, because of a player. I'm 100 percent a Jets fan because of Joe Namath. No doubt in my mind. He was one of the best. It was actually the 1965 Orange Bowl between Alabama and Texas that really got me turned onto him.

My father had told me all about the quarterback from Alabama. He told me how I had to watch this kid play—the white shoes, the big arm...the whole deal. So I watched the game, and Namath played phenomenally. Unfortunately, it ended with a 21-17 loss, as Texas stopped Namath's quarterback sneak on 4th-and-inches. But I was already hooked. Namath was my guy.

So the die was cast when he signed with the Jets in 1965. I couldn't believe it. It was then and there that I said to myself, **I'm rooting for this team. I'm rooting for this guy.** Up until that point, I hadn't had a rooting interest in football. My father didn't really have a team. So I chose the Jets at age 12 because of my hero, and I haven't looked back since. I just made that cutoff, I guess. —JB

Primo-Donna

John Primavera has done it all. Sure, he's broken a few rules in the process, but he had his reasons. "Primo" is a quality hockey fan. He rattles off names like Jean Ratelle and Billy Carroll like it's nothing. He played hockey as a youngster and in college. He once even went on a western Canadian hockey trip, stopping at games in Calgary, Winnipeg, Vancouver, and Edmonton and swung through Toronto too. The average hockey fan doesn't do something like that.

Primo is no joke. His fandom, however, is a little checkered because he has some history with each of the three Tri-State area hockey teams. Believe it or not, Primo has at one point or another—and as an adult!—been a fan of the Rangers, Islanders, and Devils. Now obviously we don't condone this type of behavior; some rules should always be followed.

Primo grew up a Rangers fan, rooting for the same team that his friends did. At that time, the Rangers were the only show in town. The Islanders and Devils were not even born yet.

When the Islanders came to fruition in 1972, Primo realized he had been hanging with the wrong crowd. These Rangers fans he had been aligned with for so many years hated the Islanders and hardly acknowledged their existence. This elitist attitude started to turn Primo off. After a few years of rooting for both teams (a blatant violation of Rule #1) he dumped the Rangers (a blatant disregard for Rule #4) because he didn't want to be aligned with their fans' arrogance.

He became a partial season-ticket holder for the Islanders. It just so happens that along with Primo, victories started coming to the Island. Nassau Coliseum soon became the home of a hockey dynasty. The Islanders won four straight Stanley Cups and Primo was there to witness them.

Except that in 1982, in the middle of the Islanders' success, the seeds were growing for another switch. You see, Primo lived in New Jersey. It was only natural that he should get tickets to the Devils. After all, the team played in East Rutherford, just a 15-minute drive from his North Jersey home.

For the second time in less than a decade, Primo was attracted to the new kid on the block. He was rooting for both the Devils and Islanders, something he still does to this day.

Let's just hope the area doesn't create another new team anytime soon. Primo has already been disenchanted twice. There's no reason to believe he wouldn't do it again.

jump ship after the discovery stage. Choosing a team because of a player is fine, as long as you stick with it. It cannot be said enough: this is a lifelong commitment!

Winning
The lure of success is always attractive. As a grown adult, someone who's made a team designation, jumping on with a winning team is called front-running. But as a youngster preparing to make a choice in team, it's perfectly legal. In fact, it's understandable. Oh, to be young again!

It's no coincidence that there are a lot of Giants and Mets fans who were born in the late '70s. The Giants and Mets were winning big in the '80s, when most of those kids were growing up. Don't be surprised to see a passel of young Yankees fans soon. You can attribute that to their most recent (late '90s) dynasty.

You'll get no complaints from us. Everybody, even young children, likes a winner. After all, why would anyone want to be associated with a loser, right? But it happens. Maybe some adults should be embarrassed for guiding their children in the direction of the Mets and Jets. If history is any barometer, it guarantees a lifetime of disappointment in the face of neighbors' consistent success. But it's up to everyone to make their own decisions. Sure, not everyone can root for the winning team, can they? There have to be losers too.

Colors and Uniforms
Maybe it's not the most scientific criterion, but plenty of sports fans have done it. They selected the Giants over the Jets because they like blue better than green. How can you blame a seven-year-old for liking the Giants if his favorite color is blue? Or if they like the Yankees because of the interlocking N and Y or those pinstripes? You can't.

Stadiums or Arenas

The stadium or arena that houses a team serves as little more than a fringe benefit to fans. Sure, it's nice to move into the new Yankee Stadium, Citi Field, or the Prudential Center. But for an adult who has an established allegiance, it won't change much, aside from, perhaps, the number of games they attend each season.

But children who are still in the process of selecting a team might be swayed by the team's house. Maybe they like the posh atmosphere of the Prudential Center. Perhaps they'll look back fondly on the Shake Shack hamburgers at Citi Field. They might choose to be a Giants fan over the Jets because it was *Giants* Stadium at the Meadowlands for so many years. These are the kinds of things that could make a difference.

One fan even admitted to us that he became a Mets fan, despite the fact that his father was a die-hard Yankees fan from the Bronx, because the ushers at Shea were nicer than the ones at Yankee Stadium. Hey, it just goes to show, everything counts when it comes to impressing youngsters.

We've also heard first-hand stories about youngsters who have chosen the Yankees or the Mets because it was their Little League team name. Hey, it happens. No complaints from us. It's as good a reason as any.

We understand that choosing a team is difficult and that there are many contributing factors that figure into a decision. But while the only concrete rule is that a single team must be selected by age 13, here are the important things to keep in mind during that selection process:

- *Stick with a local team if possible.* It's easier and less expensive than having a long-distance relationship. Plus, you might not get harassed in school as much.
- *Stay within the family.* You'll have enough other stuff to argue about over the years. Sharing interest in a team will help keep open the lines of communication with your relatives and your relationships fairly amicable. Nobody

wants to hear the same never-ending arguments over every holiday table.

- *Avoid the perennial loser and avoid a lifetime of frustration.* This is often forgotten locally. Just ask any Jets, Mets, or Islanders fan. Or anyone who's cheered for the Knicks after the Ewing Era.

- *Remember, players come and go.* Five years down the line, the player or players you can't stand probably won't have any affiliation with the team. The ones you love probably won't be there either. (See Rule #3 for more information.)

things
YANKEES FANS
love

THE LEGENDS
Ruth, Gehrig, DiMaggio,
Mantle...too many to name them all.

- *Stay away from toxic owners.* While players come and go, owners have a bit more staying power. Sometimes they (along with their families) can linger for a very, very long time. If they're screwing it up, chances are they will be for the long haul. You could be waiting a long time if you're holding out for someone to die.

RULE #3

ROOT FOR THE UNIFORM, NOT THE PLAYER

George Foster, Dave Kingman, Armando Benitez, Alexei Yashin, Blair Thomas, Charles Smith, Ed Whitson, Carl Pavano, Hideki Irabu, and Kenny Rogers all had their own vociferous detractors. They were booed relentlessly by hometown fans during their time in New York. But not one of them kept the real fans from rooting hard for their team.

things DEVILS FANS hate

WAYNE GRETZKY AND MICKEY MOUSE

The Great One once said of the Islanders, "They're putting a Mickey Mouse operation on the ice.... It's ruining hockey." The comment lingers despite their subsequent success.

Get the point? Under no circumstance is a single player more valuable than his team. Every team has bad guys, players who are unpopular, guys who get into trouble off the field. But as a fan, you're rooting for the jersey more than the individual.

Players come and go, and some are loved more than others but the team won't sign a new contract or get traded away for another one. It's why you root for the team even if it has an entire roster full of unlikable players (like the late '90s Mets, for instance). Soon enough, the Bobby Bonillas and Vince Colemans of the world will be gone, rest assured.

And just like that, the Mike Piazzas and Al Leiters of the world will swoop in and take their place. And then the next flavor of the month will arrive. True fans, however, will always remain.

RULE #4

NEVER DITCH YOUR TEAM

Never ditch your team. It's a rather simple concept, one that should never—barring incredibly limited and extenuating circumstances—be broken. It's almost impossible to justify leaving history, tradition, and loyalty behind by throwing in the towel on your team. And New York–area teams are entrenched in history and tradition. Based on loyalty, their fan bases remain colossal.

For any real New York sports fan, ditching your team is unacceptable. Absolutely inconceivable. Impossible to comprehend. Your team is your team—forever! For better or worse. Through scintillating wins and demoralizing losses. 'Til death do you part.

It doesn't matter if you're a Jets fan who has suffered through decades of minimal success or a Mets fan who has bore witness to two straight monumental collapses. You don't jump ship. You can't start rooting for the Yankees because they made the playoffs one year and the Mets didn't. (If that were the case there might be no such thing as a real Mets fan.) You don't stop rooting for the Mets because they blew a seven-game division lead with only 17 games remaining in 2007. You don't start rooting for the Giants after they win their third Super Bowl championship in 21 years, an improbable triumph in Super Bowl XLII. You don't alienate the Islanders despite the franchise's 21st-century struggles or ditch the Nets because they can't get over the hump and win an NBA title during the J-Kidd era.

Fair-weather fans ditch their teams. Phony fans jump around like it's a weekend bar crawl. Real fans are there always and forever, through thick and thin—whether it's to voice their displeasure, cling to unrealistic hope, or celebrate a championship. The ultimate New York supporters never leave their teams.

Mets fans who have been there from the beginning experienced a 120-loss season in 1962—the worst year in MLB history, unless you count the 1899 Cleveland Spiders' 20–134 finish. The Cleveland *who*? Exactly. The infantile years of the Mets also saw 100-plus losses in five of their first six seasons. During the one "good" year in that span, they surged to a 66–95 mark. Jets fans have suffered 40 years without a Super Bowl appearance, enduring one rebuilding phase after the next. Rangers fans waited 54 years between Stanley Cup victories. In those decades were years of demoralizing playoff losses. Yet real fans (including us) remain onboard with nary a waver. They still support their favorite team up until the day they die. To the true blue New York fan, this is nothing more than fulfilling the most basic obligation. To do anything else is uncivilized.

Why Stick With Your Team?

Chance of Ultimate Glory

Almost every fan has at one point or another contemplated surrendering. Surely the thought had to cross Mets fans' minds after the team's historic collapse in the final month of the 2007 season. For the cynics and natural pessimists like us, there doesn't even need to be a drastic disappointment to precipitate doubt. We just constantly threaten to leave for good. And there is nothing wrong with that. It's one thing to invoke threats, and quite another to act on them. We might talk tough, but we would never go through with it. Heck, we wouldn't even seriously consider it.

Giving up on your team, for however little time, would make it impossible to fully enjoy the glory of the ultimate celebration. The prospect of a championship is what keeps us going. Somehow, someday, the Knicks, Jets, Nets, Mets, and Islanders will *all* go on that magical run. It will make all the struggles and bad memories evaporate in one fell swoop.

It happened for Rangers fans in 1994. After five and a half decades of patient ardor, fans got what they'd been waiting for. The team finally exorcised the demons haunting them and won the Stanley Cup. For many, it was the greatest sports moment of the decade, and for some, their sporting lives. Fans felt the same sort of jubilation when the Mets and Giants captured titles in 1986 and when the Yankees won in 1996.

I know what you're thinking: *Why can't it happen to the Knicks sometime before I die?* Chances are, if you hang around long enough, it will. Triumph, no matter how improbable, is inevitable. Or, for the glass-half-empties out there, the chances are that time will come around when you're gone—the very next year.

The beauty is that you never know when the improbable championship run is going to happen. That's why you have to watch every season. Nobody thought the Giants were going to win Super Bowl XLII, especially after they started the season 0–2. Real Giants fans never seriously contemplated ditching the team. Idle threats, maybe—but with supreme emphasis on "idle."

As for those fans who quickly jumped off the bandwagon before returning later, who needs them? Fans like that are frauds. They probably break 80 percent of the rules in this book. They might have enjoyed the Giants' surprising success in 2007, but not in the same manner as those who stuck with the team during the early-season struggles. In the end, experiencing the turbulent times—the Eli Manning bashing, the stupid interceptions, his quivering lip and confused looks—made the joy of victory that much more exhilarating for the true Giants fan. It made all the previous difficult losses (the 24–21 loss to Tennessee the previous year when Mathias Kiwanuka let go of Vince Young behind the line of scrimmage on fourth down) and playoff failures (how can you forget Trey Junkin's bad snap against the 49ers in the '03 playoffs, when the Giants blew a 24-point second-half lead?) worthwhile. It made being a true fan worthwhile.

It's in the Blood
Your father was a fan. Your mother was a fan. Your father's father was a fan. How could you end the family tradition? How could you even consider not passing the fanaticism to your children and grandchildren? Past generations

things
RANGERS FANS
love

RON DUGUAY'S MULTI
MULLET
You know you loved it.

would be rolling in their graves if ties were inexplicably and completely severed.

Traditionally, fandom is instilled in children when they are easily influenced. For many, it's ingrained in them when they are infants and becomes one hallmark of their childhoods. Some of the best memories are watching or attending a game with your father or grandfather. We've all heard the stories before: "Remember that time we saw Stephane Matteau score the game-winning goal against Martin Brodeur and the Devils in double overtime to send the Rangers to the Stanley Cup in 1994?" "Remember when Brett Favre took a dive to give Michael Strahan the single-season sack record in 2001?" "What about when Derek Jeter became Mr. November and hit that home run off Byung-Hyun Kim in the 10ᵗʰ inning of a World Series game in 2001?" "Remember when Jumbo Elliot caught that touchdown pass for the Jets at about 1:00 AM during their Monday Night Miracle win over the Dolphins in 2000?"

These pictures get deposited in the memory bank forever. They are stories that are told time and again when the family gets together for holidays or other special occasions. They are the unforgettable moments that make being a fan so rewarding. It doesn't matter whether you were there in the stadium, sitting in the living room with family, or at a bar with friends. We've all been there, jumping up and down, hugging family members or perfect strangers after a great play or victory. By the same token, we've sat sulking in a demoralizing loss. The important part is we're sharing something as a group, and it's a huge reason real fans don't ditch their team: togetherness. Disassociating with your team would be like cutting off the entire family. You could never do that! Family won't let family go.

Most fans want to give their children a choice (see Rule #5). And that's fine. They can choose any team they want. Most of the time, though, they will thankfully follow in your footsteps anyway, allowing you to enjoy these special moments together.

The Long-Range Jets Commuter

Hayden Bluth loves his Jets. He loves them so much that he moved back from Denver after just a few months, in part because he couldn't bear the thought of missing the Jets' home games. After flying to New York for the 2004 season opener, Hayden went back to Colorado, packed his bags, filled the trunk, and returned in time for the second home game of the season.

This shouldn't be surprising. Hayden is as loyal to the Jets as you can get. He never misses a game, no matter where in the world he is, whether it means traveling back to New Jersey or watching it on TV. He's also the kind of fan that, no matter the circumstance, believes the team is going to finally turn it around and be successful. He's the ultimate eternal optimist. Even during what turned out to be a 4-12 campaign in '05, Hayden had an intricate scenario mapped out about how the Jets could make the postseason. And this was at a December game in New England, when they were 2-9 and had two contests with the Pats left on the schedule. Now **that's** extreme!

Clearly, his loyal dedication to the team can't be questioned. Especially when you take into consideration that Hayden attended a remarkable 39 of 40 regular-season Jets home games (plus the Jets' one home playoff contest) from 1997-2001 when he was a student—at the University of Maryland. At 220 miles each way and 40 games, Hayden traveled approximately 17,600 miles those five years just to see his Jets. And that's not counting the road contests he attended.

And the one game he missed? Don't worry, it was unintentional. Hayden, a freshman at the time, had planned to take an Amtrak train to New Jersey for a game against the Baltimore Ravens. A driving rainstorm, however, delayed train service. There was no way he could get to New Jersey in time for the game. Instead, he rushed back to the College Park bars and caught every snap of the Jets' 19-16 overtime victory.

After that experience, Hayden elected to make the 3$^{1}/_{2}$ to 4-hour drive north instead of taking the train. And most of the time, he left at 5:30 AM—after a night out at the bar, no less, when he sometimes didn't get to bed until at least 2 AM. His internal clock would make sure he was awake and on the road early. Hayden was too afraid to miss another game. Now that's true loyalty.

Loyalty

Loyalty is important, especially to New Yorkers. It's the reason you don't sell out your family or friends. It's why individuals are trusted and respected. It's why you don't all of a sudden pull a Johnny Damon and join the enemy. Then again, Damon at least had a reasonable excuse. He was paid millions of dollars to jump across enemy lines. As a fan, you don't have that viable excuse. You don't get a monetary reward for joining the enemy. It's pride and obligation.

Loyalty is what sets fans apart from players. It is the most vital trait for any real sports fan to possess. Players have a job to do, plain and simple. Being a fan is a different animal. It's a conscious choice, a devotion, a part of yourself that you sacrifice to a cause—a lifelong commitment.

Without loyalty, the Rangers or Knicks wouldn't have anyone in the stands. Both teams have been inconsistent at best, putrid at worst—but they also have two of the most loyal fan bases in all of sports. We can actually argue that Rangers and Knicks fans are the most loyal in all of sports. Most fans around the country would have jumped off both teams' bandwagons and picked more exciting, successful teams to support a long time ago. Can you imagine New York filled with Detroit Red Wings and San Antonio Spurs fans?

Luckily, turning tail is not in a true New York fan's blood. Electing to stop rooting for your favorite team would be akin to telling your best friend it's over because he's not good at picking up girls. Talk about a low blow. Sure, you would love to see him do well, but if he doesn't, you still have your friend's back, don't you? You're still willing to serve as his wingman and help the cause, aren't you? At no point should you completely give up hope for your friend—or your favorite team.

The Inexcusable

Every team has been through turbulent times. Two games into the 2007 season, the Giants were struggling. Many were already

FAN TIP

If you're really frustrated with the team's direction, take a hiatus.
Just don't latch on with a different organization.

calling for coach Tom Coughlin's dismissal. Eli's failings were plastered across the sports pages. People were questioning if he could avoid the Brett Favre-like miscues and mature into an adequate quarterback. No one was holding their breath.

Manning, Coughlin, and most Giants fans persevered, and the team went on to win the Super Bowl. As a fan, you need to persevere too. Lack of success, poor management (yes, we're talking about Mr. Dolan again), and unlikable players are unnerving problems, but never are they grounds for abandonment. No retreat, no surrender. A true fan has to go the distance if he ever expects his team to do the same.

Poor Performance

Plenty of teams perform poorly. Some, like the Jets, have just done it a little more often than most over the past four decades. For them, losing is an annual ritual. They torture everyone, from the die-hards to the fringe fans. Other teams, like the Mets, just seem to break your heart more than most. They are always oh-so-close, yet so far away. Regardless of the type of failure your team might deliver, you as a fan need to hang in there.

Remember, there is only one team that wins the final game of the season. Losing is a part of sports and an inevitability in life. It's an affliction everybody must endure at some point or another—even in Boston, where everything seems to be going well more often than not these days.

Bear in mind that New York has experienced its fair share of success. Every New York Metropolitan–area team has made the playoffs some time in the 21st century. There are no astounding playoff droughts. Maybe there have been demoralizing playoff losses (the Mets' 2006 National League Championship Series against St. Louis comes to mind), but it could be worse. You could be rooting for, say, the Kansas City Royals, Detroit Lions, or Cleveland Indians.

If you're out the second things turn sour, you're nothing more than a fair-weather fan. And there really is nothing worse and less respectable than a fair-weather fan, is there? When teams constantly lose, these so-called fans stop supporting the team. Corporate boxes go unfilled. The die-hards, sitting way up in the nosebleeds every game, remain—cheering as loudly and proudly as they do during a superlative season.

Rangers fans paid thousands of dollars each year for their upper-deck seats—even during the seasons when they were inept, had the highest payroll in the sport, and went nine years without making the playoffs. If you go to Madison Square Garden, you'll see the real Knicks fans who still do the same. Courtside seats for Knicks games can cost season-ticket holders six figures each year. They still pay it. Why? Spike Lee and company are not fair-weather fans. They're real fans who are willing to stick with their team through thick and thin.

Sticking around for the long haul—and especially the bad times—makes victory taste even sweeter. Ask the Rangers fans who waited 54 years, the ones who hung around during

Losing Doesn't Scare Me

When the Mets came around in '62, I was nine years old. I looked at it as a great opportunity: If I followed them, I would be there for everything, right from the beginning. It was a fresh start. I knew that if I was a Mets fan I would be there to see the first everything—the first pitch, the first home run, the first championship. Unfortunately, that also included the first 100-plus-loss season, followed by three more in a row. But I never contemplated leaving. Never.

The Mets were my team and that was that. I made that decision and was willing to stick with it no matter what happened. I knew eventually it would get better. They weren't going to lose 120 games each season. Were they? Fortunately, they didn't. Seven years later, they won the World Series. —JB all the sour times. Those fans endured heart-wrenching playoff losses and choke jobs. But if you ask them, they would all do it again. In the end, the damage done by all those losses and poor performances was nothing compared to the elation of getting that Stanley Cup championship.

Poor Management
The owner is cheap, the general manager is an idiot, and the team president doesn't know how to run a business. Join the club. That pretty much describes the sentiment of sports fans across the country.

things
KNICKS FANS
love

DUNK CHAMPIONS
At least the Knicks have won something. Kenny Walker and Nate Robinson have both taken home the crown.

More often than not, fans feel that their team is mismanaged and run inefficiently and incorrectly.

James Dolan is the prime example. The Cablevision boss doesn't know anything about basketball or hockey, yet he runs the Knicks and Rangers.

For years, Glen Sather was a disaster as the Rangers' general manager. Ditto Isiah Thomas as the Knicks' president. Both men were despised by significant fractions of their teams' fan base. And for good reason. Isiah oversaw the worst period in Knicks history, when they failed to make the playoffs in any of his five seasons with the team. The Rangers missed the playoffs during the first eight years of Sather's tenure.

Leon Hess meant well too. He just didn't know how to run a professional football franchise effectively, and the Jets suffered as a result of his inadequacies. They failed to make a Super Bowl during his lifetime.

Yankees owner George Steinbrenner always wanted to win. He just didn't always go about achieving success the best way possible. Too many times he went after the aging name and overpaid players at the expense of young prospects.

Mets owner Fred Wilpon has signed off on more bad deals than just about anyone in the history of baseball. He was responsible for wasting money on busts like Mo Vaughn and Roberto Alomar, among others.

The Islanders have been inconsistent at best through out most of Charles Wang's reign. He's fired coaches and general managers at an alarming rate. Yet he allowed general manager Mike Millbury to hang around and make bad decisions for years.

Every owner has foibles, and no matter what team you root for, you're going to complain about them. But keep in mind that you don't root for the owner, GM, or team president. Sure, they *are* part of the team, but they're not out there on the playing field. Your job as a fan is to root for the players. You root for the colors and logo. You don't root for or against a general manager or owner.

Although it may not always seem like it, management eventually comes and goes. Believe it or not, George Steinbrenner was not always the owner of tho Yankees. Unfortunately, changes upstairs don't come as often as they do on the field, rink, or court. But no matter how long it takes, you have to wait it out. Right now it might seem impossible to fathom, but there will be a day Dolan is not running the Knicks and Rangers. Stick with it, Rangers and Knicks fans. There will probably be a celebrating parade when it happens.

Conversely, it is possible you're stuck with an owner like Dolan for quite some time. Too bad. Fight through it. It's not a valid reason to ditch your team. Even the dumbest, most incompetent owners will have their day. Hey, even with Sather and Dolan running the show, the Rangers made the Eastern Conference Finals in 2007. That is tangible proof that you can win with even the most clueless blockheads running the show. So make sure you're there when it happens. True fans have nothing to worry about.

Unlikable Players

Alex Rodriguez is the latest in a long line of hometown players despised by a faction of his own teams' fans. It doesn't matter that he won the MVP, hit 54 homers, and knocked in 156 runs in 2007 or that he was instrumental during their '09 playoff run. There are Yankee fans out there who will never like A-Rod. They will always detest him, especially when he fails in the clutch. Yet, the real fans, despite what they might think of him as a player, still root for the Yankees.

Out of the Area

Go anywhere around the world, and you can bet your bottom dollar you can find a Yankees fan. They live everywhere, from Maine to California, Europe, and Asia. You can find Giants fans in Washington, D.C. Rangers fans in Canada. Islanders fans in New England. Jets fans in Florida.

Even if you live in a different town, city, or time zone, following your favorite New York team is no big deal. Ever hear of DirectTV or the Internet? How about *SportsCenter*? Even if you're electronically and technologically incompetent, you can still support the team you grew up loving—even if you're out of the area. It would be flat-out wrong to start rooting for a different team just because you moved. Would you cheat on your partner just because you were in a long-distance relationship? Of course not, not if you were really in love. Besides, long-distance relationships in sports are far more successful than they are in romance.

things
ISLANDERS FANS
hate

BRYAN TROTTIER,
RANGERS COACH
He just looked out of place
near a Rangers logo.

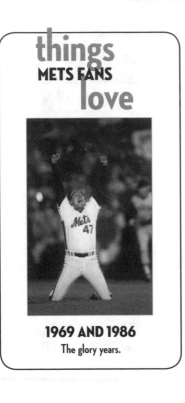

things
METS FANS
love

1969 AND 1986
The glory years.

You don't just inherit a new team upon relocation to a new city. The Welcome Wagon doesn't drop it off at your door when you move. Even before you could watch the Yankees and the YES Network from anywhere in the United States, moving to a new city was not a valid reason to change allegiances. And it doesn't matter if you've lived in the secondary city longer than the place where you were raised. Your home is always your home. If you grew up a Jets, Giants, Mets, Yankees, Knicks, Nets, Devils, Rangers, or Islanders fan, they should always be your team, regardless of where you find yourself.

Breaking up is hard to do, but sometimes it's necessary. Following are the very few reasons a true sports fan can justify leaving his team.

The Excusable

You Work for the Team

Being a fan is one thing, but making your living from them is another. For most of us working stiffs, our fandom doesn't produce income—although a lot of people out there probably wish it could. This, of course, leaves out working for the Knicks, where you would be required to work under buffoons like Dolan and Thomas. A lot of fans (us included) would probably opt for a root canal rather than sit through a meeting with that brilliant tandem.

For the most part, if you are fortunate enough to land a job with a sports franchise or university and it's a good opportunity, you will accept the offer. But in accepting that job offer, you are also obligated to change your allegiance. It might be painful, but if you grew up a Giants fan and are now working for the Cowboys, Eagles, or Redskins, you have to do it. To a die-hard Islanders fan who now works for the Rangers, tough break. Working is higher on the priority list than rooting interest.

The same holds true for family and very close friends of players, coaches, and management. You have to support the people close to you. Consider the parents of Yankees catcher Jose Molina. Molina has two brothers, Yadier and Bengie, who also play professionally. Their parents are required to root for all three of the teams that employ their sons—even if two are the Mets and Yankees. As a parent, it's impossible not to want your children to succeed. Over the course of their careers, the Molina family may well root for half of the teams in the league at some point or another. They can at least take comfort in the fact that they have three times the chance of seeing a winner in any given year.

Friends of players, coaches, and management don't live with the same rules, though. They can't jump ship. Sure, they can root for their friend's individual happiness and success, but they should also stay true to their own team. A friend's team can be their second-favorite team, but it should always take a backseat to the original.

Your Team Leaves the City
This is also a no-brainer for fans. You were jilted and left standing at the altar by the love of your life. What do you do? You don't go

**things
JETS FANS
hate**

BELICHICK
Wrote on a napkin:
"I resign as HC of the NYJ."
Thanks for the one day, buddy.

chasing around the country for someone who rejected you, do you? Of course not. You don't go lock yourself in the house and cry all day and night either. You pick yourself up off the ground, look yourself in the mirror, and start over in search of new happiness.

The Dodgers and Giants both split for the West Coast in the late '50s. When they did, the also abandoned generations of fans in New York. So many young Dodgers fans could no longer see their heroes, the great Duke Snyder and Sandy Koufax, on a daily basis. Giants fans couldn't watch the exploits of the amazing Willie Mays. They hadn't given up on their team, their team had given up on them. So they did what the situation dictated: they looked for a new team. Soon enough, along came the Mets. The perfect rebound for the abandoned baseball lover.

The line has to be drawn somewhere, and as a fan, you cannot be expected to remain loyal to a team that shows no loyalty to you. If a team leaves you, it's okay to move on.

PART THREE

ENEMY MINE

---

*Note: The term **enemy** in this chapter is used to describe fans of rival teams.*

RULE #5

ASSOCIATE WITH, MARRY, OR RAISE THE ENEMY—ONLY IF YOU MUST

In a perfect world, Yankees fans would marry Yankees fans and Mets fans would marry Mets fans. There would be no mixed marriages at all in this regard, far fewer fights for the coveted remote control, and little-to-no use for picture-in-picture.

There wouldn't be any comingling either. Rangers fans would hang out at bars in Manhattan, Islanders fans at establishments on Long Island, and Devils fans would stick to their own watering holes in New Jersey. Everyone would stay where they seemingly belong and the populace would get along perfectly. There would be no such thing as enemies. Rivalries wouldn't pose any issues. There would be far fewer barroom brawls and much less heated banter. This is a pacifist's utopia.

How much fun would that be? Not so much for New York sports fans. It would be a scary sports world if everything was perfect and everyone in it was happy. Think about it: it would be far from Never Never-Land. There would be no rivalries and a lot more ties. It sounds reminiscent of the new-style grade school gym classes where there are no losers and dodgeball is out of the question. Everybody wins, yippee!

Thankfully that type of philosophy would never fly with New Yorkers. New York is the world's fastest and most demanding city—and, fortunately, it isn't sports-segregated. There are winners and losers in every game, unless it's hockey or the MLB All-Star Game. (Thanks, Bud.)

Fans', players', coaches', and management's desire to win is what makes it all worthwhile. It's what makes rivalries intense battles. After all, isn't that what sports is at its root: a contest? In competition, there are losers and there are winners. That's reality, even if teachers and parents try to obscure that inevitability.

You might not recognize it: the enemy is everywhere. They are in the office where you work, the restaurant where you're eating, behind you in the grocery line. Sometimes they're right under your nose. Sometimes they're even in your home. That's right—have a couple drinks and next thing you know they might be sleeping in your bed. It sounds scary, but it has been known to happen. You could literally be sleeping with the enemy.

Proof that the enemy is always lurking will reveal itself when you are most vulnerable. Take, for instance, the Red Sox fans who popped out at every corner in New York after they rallied from a 3–0 series deficit against the Yankees in the 2004 ALCS. Sure, we knew that there were Boston fans among us. But Red Sox fans were like Gremlins after that series—they just kept multiplying. They filled Yankee Stadium during the Game 7 demolition.

No matter where you are, there is no such thing as a safe haven. There are Red Sox fans living in New York, and Yankees fans in Boston; Phillies fans in Queens, and Mets fans in Philadelphia. There are Dolphins and Cowboys fans in the Tri-State area (an inordinate amount, unfortunately) but there is also more than a fair share of Giants and Jets fans in South Florida.

A Jets fan and a Giants fan married? Oh my! The jury is still out on which team the kid will root for.
Photo courtesy of Allison Brennan

(It just might be that the latter are all over the age of 80 and circumspect in their, shall we say, veracity of allegiance.)

New York, more than any other city, is a melting pot. Its diversity is well-known—*everybody* in New York is in the minority in one way or another. You can find a fan of just about every team in the world living somewhere in the Metropolitan area, and that includes the South Sydney Rabbitohs, the most successful Australian Rugby League team, and the Kidderminster Harriers, a relatively unknown, low-level English soccer club. Trust us, search hard enough and ye shall find, especially in a city as multicultural as New York. Just head to one of the city's Irish or English pubs on the weekend and you'll see for yourself.

The overabundance of Cowboys, Dolphins, and Bulls fans may be irksome to local fans. Particularly when they become loud and annoying when their teams do well. They emerge like

Sleeping with the Enemy

Andrew Nadler is one in a large group of mixed-marriage New York sports fans. He is a die-hard Mets fan and his wife, Rebecca, is a Yankees fan. In two-team (or in some cases three-team) cities, this phenomenon isn't that uncommon.

You learn to live with the other's "shortcoming." It might cause a few arguments here or there, but it's nothing that cannot be overcome. Andrew and Rebecca are living proof. Sure, the in-house rivalry makes for some uncomfortable moments, such as when she comes home to find him watching the Mets, or when the two teams meet in the biannual Subway Series. Still, they survive.

It often helps when one party's obsession far outweighs the other. Andrew tips the scales in this household. The Mets stuff is spread out all over, while the Yankees paraphernalia is relegated to a certain room. Hey, whatever works for them

Still, the ultimate test awaits them when they have children. What will they do then? Andrew intends to make sure he buys unlimited Mets paraphernalia for the child to try and influence the decision at a young age. "Gotta make sure they don't step foot in Yankee Stadium for a while," he said. "Gotta go to Citi Field at least five or six times first for me to have a chance." When the time comes, we'll see what Rebecca has to say about that.

cockroaches in the night, getting in your face and bragging about their teams. Then, as quickly as they appeared, they vanish during the turbulent times. Where were the Cowboys, Bulls, and Dolphins fans in the early 21st century? They must have been on vacation.

The enemy comes in a variety of forms: friends, coworkers, acquaintances.... The enemy can be your husband or wife, boyfriend or girlfriend, your parents or children. Anything is possible—even if not ideal. Unfortunately, these mistakes can happen. And they seem to occur more than one would think.

At nearly any game, be it the Subway Series or a Knicks-Nets contest, you can pick out a husband-wife combo in the stands supporting their respective teams. This conflict creates plenty of dilemmas, none more pertinent than when kids are involved: which team will the children support? Which parent will they join and which will they betray? How hard should they be pushed toward one team or the other?

It's a sticky situation, but parents who support different teams should try to be neutral when it comes to guiding their kids. Sure, they can put in their two cents, offer their opinions, and maybe provide an authoritative nudge (starting from the day of birth), but in the end, it is probably best to let children make their own decisions.

Then again, if you marry someone who does not have any team affiliations, your spouse should inherit your allegiances. Your spouse should begin rooting for your team immediately. That is a gimme. Our wives thankfully obliged. Why "thankfully"? It's all for the good of the marriage. We're happy, they're happy. Just imagine how awkward it would be if your spouse rooted against you just for the hell of it. That alone would be grounds for divorce. It would be weird, confrontational, and uncomfortable. It would create unnecessary tension and additional arguments. Nobody needs that.

Usually, you want your spouse to be happy. The last thing you desire is someone sitting next to you basking in a victory

My Daughter, My Yankees Fan?

I'm obviously a Mets fan. I don't hide that. And, yes, my daughter is a Yankees fan. After my wife and I split up in 1988, she moved with the kids to her home state, Massachusetts. Our children have always been sports fans because of me. Both my daughters were fans of the Jets, no way around that. But even though I had taken my daughter, Sam, to some Mets games, it never really stuck with her. Growing up in Massachusetts, she had a front-row seat to the obnoxiousness of Red Sox fans. They drove her crazy. So she started rooting for the Yankees to drive **them** crazy.

I'm not thrilled about it (of course, I wish she were a Mets fan) but it makes some sense. I'd like to think that if I'd been there to keep her focused on the Mets, we'd be rooting for them together. But as it turns out, she became a fervent baseball fan in 2001 and the Yankees, who had won four of the past five years, didn't win again until 2009. It must be the Benigno karma. And as far as I'm concerned, if that's the case, then fine. —JB while you wallow in defeat—especially when you're supposed to be a harmonious team. So what better way to create marital harmony than by rooting for your spouse's favorite team to win—especially if you never had a real allegiance in the first place? Given the option, you would rather not have an enemy right there in your own backyard. Trust us, it's better for both sides involved.

Unfortunately, not every marriage happens this way. And in certain cases, it can be tenable. In fact, if a spouse is a true fan unwilling to break an original allegiance, that should be respected.

RULE #6

AVOID THE ENEMY WHEN NECESSARY

There are certain times when it's best to be alone. Like Tony Montana when he wants you to say hello to his "little friend" or Tony Soprano when he's gone off his Prozac prescription. Sometimes it's just best to stay away from others. Otherwise, there could be very big trouble.

Enemies take note: stay away. There is no animal more volatile than a New York sports fans after a bad loss. Having Mets and Yankees fans in the same room after the 2000 Subway Series was a combustible mix. Ditto Rangers and Devils fans following their heated 1994 playoff series that ended on Stephane Matteau's Game 7 overtime goal. The Rangers went on to win the Stanley Cup and end a 54-year drought thanks to that goal.

When Alex Rodriguez's pop-up caromed off the heel of Luis Castillo's glove and fell harmlessly to the ground in the ninth inning of the Mets' most memorable 2009 loss to the Yankees, the last thing in the world any Mets fan needed was a Yankees fan in his face. It's times like these that fans need to head off to a secluded area, power down the cell phone, and temporarily

Most Valuable Spouse

It takes a special breed to handle sports fans like us. It's certainly not easy, that's for sure. To be married to a real New York sports fan, you need to be one of the best. Tremendous. Stellar, even.

Terry Benigno fits this description. She knew what she was in for before marrying me, a lunatic sports fan, and she still made the move without hesitation. And that was before this sports obsession was part of the job, too. That says a lot. She knew her future husband was passionate. That was made very clear from the beginning. It had to be clear if the marriage had any chance of working. But there were still some surprises along the way. Terry had no idea just how important being a fan was going to become.

What Terry found was that she married into more than a family. She was also taking on the Mets, Jets, Knicks, and Rangers. It was a shock to the system. Still, it's part of the package when marrying a die-hard. Your life takes a new shape, molded around the daily schedule of the team.

Now, years later, she's become inured to the lifestyle. She can't even imagine what a Sunday without football (and bloodcurdling screams) would be like. Now she mentions the **Heidi** Game offhandedly; she knows 1986 as surely as 1969. She has seamlessly embraced the lifestyle, and she is now a die-hard New York sports fan too. Now that's a perfect wife! —JB

cease any and all interaction with society, particularly fans from the opposing team.

Those hard losses are tough to take, but every team experiences them. The Knicks had the Reggie Miller "choke" game. The Nets blew a nine-point lead in Game 6 of the '03 Finals. The Mets had the Castillo drop and countless September defeats in '07 and '08 that had fans pulling their hair out. The Mets had their Game 7 loss to the St. Louis Cardinals in the '04 NLCS too. The Yankees had Game 7 of the '01 World Series and the Luis Gonzalez bloop and the '03 ALCS Game 7 blowout loss to Boston, capping off their slide from a 3–0 series lead. The Devils allowed two goals in 91 seconds to blow Game 7 of their first-round series against Carolina in 2009. The Jets had the "fake spike game" and countless other unthinkable losses. The

Giants had the '03 playoff debacle in San Francisco when they blew a 24-point lead before failing to complete the snap and hold on a game-winning field goal attempt.

Just enumerating these games is enough to send New York fans into hibernation—possibly even the asylum. These are the situations that send fans running for the hills. And for good reason. Nothing positive comes from communication with the enemy during times like these. That's why New York fans need to avoid rival—and particularly crosstown rival—fans during moments like this:

Avoid the enemy...

...after a bad loss

Having to listen to anyone at this moment is tantamount to being locked in a room with Fran Drescher squawking in your ear. When all you want is some time to collect your thoughts, cool down, digest what just happened, and begin the recuperation process, it's impossible with a major distraction in the room. A confrontation with the enemy elicits the exact opposite effect. You just get more frustrated, irritated, and risk blowing up. This is why caller ID was invented.

...prior to a big game

It's just not the time for a chat. It's time to begin preparation, time to get into the proper frame of mind and assume your position, whether it's in front of the television or in the stadium.

FAN TIP

Don't ever call an enemy fan when they are watching an NFL game involving their team. That's a big mistake.

Most fans have their set pregame routines. Nattering with the enemy moments before a big game, when your nerves are already raw, could produce a volatile situation in seconds flat. It's like going backstage and heckling an actor moments before he begins a scene. At that moment, it's all about being in your own headspace. Visitors—especially unsympathetic ones—are unwelcome.

**things
RANGERS FANS
hate**

JAMES DOLAN
As reviled by hockey fans
as he is by basketball fans.

...when your rival just won a championship or title

Mike Tyson just landed a punch in your gut and then kicked you several times after you fell to the ground. That's how you feel after your rival just won a championship. You will be eating crow plenty in the ensuing days, months and years, but the moment afterward is the tenderest. Avoid the enemy at all costs. You'll be the happier for it.

...during key moments in a game

Shame on you! It's like answering a phone call at 1:30 PM on a football Sunday. It's unconscionable if your team is playing. Anyone who commits such a gaffe should be stripped of his Man Card.

RULE #7

DON'T BE "THAT GUY" DURING AND AFTER LOSSES

The NFL mandates a 10-minute cool-down period for players before the media is granted access to the clubhouse. Major League Baseball, the NHL, and the NBA have similar restrictions. New York sports fans need even more time than that. Why take 10 minutes when you could have 10 years? And then some? Of course, we'd love to never hear about that crushing loss or that bonehead play after it happens, but realistically, that's not an option. Particularly in a town as media-saturated as New York. You're gonna see the play. So do yourself a favor and take at least one hour to digest what just happened to your team.

An hour is ample time to collect your thoughts and regain rationality. It's enough time to simmer down and be coherent again. That hour is vital to the maintenance of many relationships. It can potentially quell volatile situations and prevent unnecessary blowups. The sports fan who calls to rub it in before that hour has elapsed is "that guy." Nobody wants to be that guy. So back off. Don't be that guy. Don't call your friend the second after the game ends to rub in the latest loss. The annoying friend or relative who wants to tell you his team just won a championship is asking for it. After all, it's not as if you don't already know.

RULE #8

DON'T GO OVERBOARD WITH THE TRASH TALK

Mothers have nothing to do with sports arguments. Neither do spouses. Name-calling needs to be kept to a minimum. Anything the slightest bit racist, sexist, prejudiced, or discriminatory is especially verboten. Don't even dare go there.

That said, insulting a friend's intelligence is fair game. Same with their height, weight, athletic ability, bad breath, and proclivity for unattractive or overweight women.

The Dos and Don'ts of Associating with the Enemy
The Dos
Do trash-talk.
Where would sports be without it? It happens all the time between rival fans and allows for fun, spirited conversation. But remember to always be prudent, because what goes around comes around. So don't keep piling it on after the Yankees beat the Mets in the Subway Series. One day—maybe even sometime this century, before we die—the result will be reversed.

things
JETS FANS
hate

GIANTS STADIUM
Playing in a stadium named after another team is downright degrading. It also happens to be in New Jersey. A New York team playing in N.J. is irritating.

Do sleep with the enemy.
Never, ever, turn down the advances of someone that you're interested in because of her allegiance. Some things are more important than sports—or at least they should be.

Do marry the enemy.
Only a truly sick individual would refuse to marry someone because of her allegiance to a team. But there are definitely some sickos out there. Let's just hope that you're not one of them.

Do avoid the enemy when necessary.
Sometimes you just need some "me time." Usually it's after bad losses or a ridiculous play. But it can also be necessary after a

particularly draining win. Whenever you need it, take it. That's your prerogative.

The Don'ts

Don't rub it in immediately after a bad loss.
Only the most annoying, inconsiderate human beings stoop to this level. But we're willing to wager that every one of you has that one friend who does it consistently. Throwing salt in a fresh wound is the lowest of the low—so remember that the next time you're tempted to open your mouth. Don't be that guy. Obey the one-hour grace period before going in for the kill. That extra hour at least allows the mourner some time to loosen the noose.

Don't call during games.
Nothing is quite as egregious as the previous transgression, but calling your enemy during the game is still pretty bad. It's a

The Annoying Enemy

There are some who say Shaun Joseph is responsible for the Yankees' late-'90s dynasty. Who is Shaun Joseph, you ask? He's not a player, coach, or front-office executive. In fact, he has no affiliation with the Yankees. Shaun is little more than a die-hard Mets fan with Eddie Mush-like luck. He also happens to be "that guy."

Shaun's contribution to the Yankees dynasty dates back to 1996, when they won their first championship in 18 years. For a while, it looked like the Yankees would have to wait a little bit longer. That's until Shaun violated the rules of associating with the enemy and committed two, maybe three, simultaneous don'ts.

This lifelong Mets fan made an ill-timed phone call. With the Yankees trailing 6-0 in Game 4 and down 2-1 in the series, it didn't look good for the Bronx Bombers. So Shaun picked up the phone, dialed his friend—a Yankees fan—and declared the World Series over. A six-run rally capped by a Jim Leyritz homer followed, and the Yankees were on their way to three straight wins and four championships in five years.

Some might say it was Shaun Joseph that mushed that game and series and unleashed a dynasty.

100-percent guarantee: that fan doesn't want to hear from you. Be patient. There's an entire week to rehash anything and everything.

Don't try to convert the enemy. It's not going to happen with any real fan, so don't bother wasting your time. In fact, it's more likely to backfire. It's akin to attempting to convince your friend not to marry the girl he loves. The inevitable result is resentment and, in some cases, the end of the friendship.

Don't spawn the enemy. Sometimes you can't control it, but if at all possible, try for your children to follow in your footsteps. Do what you can—without forcing it down their throats, of course—to steer them in the proper direction.

things
YANKEES FANS
love

YOGI-ISMS

"Nobody goes there anymore. It's too crowded." "If you see a fork in the road, take it." "I didn't really say everything I said."

PART FOUR

GEARING UP

RULE #9

YOU MUST OWN ONE PIECE OF PARAPHERNALIA FOR YOUR TEAM

Any fan, no matter his level of dedication or financial situation, should own at least one piece of paraphernalia. It really isn't too much to ask. Just have something, *anything*. It could be a hat, jersey, T-shirt, jacket, tie, scarf, bandanna, cufflinks, bag, glove, bat, bobblehead doll, pen, mug, pennant, towel, plaque, key chain, money clip, Mr. Potato Head, bib, puzzle, lighter, scented candle, pendant, ring, putting mat, golf ball, head cover, thermos, clock, Christmas ornament, lunch box, wallet, dartboard, dog leash, or choker. The list could go on forever—which just goes to show that there's something for everybody. The teams and leagues will seemingly throw their logos on anything, so long as it correlates to increased revenue. Heck, they even make personalized team caskets and tombstones these days, proving there's something for every fan in life *or* death.

While we're not necessarily advocating a team casket or tombstone (it seems rather excessive, even to sports-obsessed freaks like us), every real New York fan should have a little something containing their favorite team's logo. Most of us have plenty of stuff.

Almost every Yankees and Mets fan seems to have a hat with their respective team's interlocking NY emblazoned on the front. Consider a New York baseball game. We guesstimate that about 60 percent of the crowd is sporting the home team's hat.

The best part, especially during the summer, is that it's practical. It can help keep you cool and prevent you from looking like a tomato after a full day in the sun. Plus, it's easy, convenient, financially reasonable, and a sensible way to make a statement for your team. It's a symbol of your loyalty.

Hats are required fan gear for any sport, but only in baseball is the hat a part of the team's official uniform. If you sport your Mets cap at Citi Field, you're wearing an identical version to the one on Jose Reyes' head. It allows fans to feel the part. Almost everybody, (and especially kids) likes to play dress up. While a real jersey can often set you back hundreds of dollars, a real Mets or Yankees cap is an affordable option. At $30 on the teams' websites, it's cheaper than the dough you'd spend for a ticket in the upper deck, and the hot dog, several beers, and french fries you'd eat during a trip at the stadium. It also lasts much longer.

When it comes to football, a jersey is probably the top preference for Jets and Giants fans—that or a T-shirt, sweatshirt, or jacket is a sartorial requirement for game days. Head to Giants Stadium on a winter afternoon and the stands are either filled with blue or green.

A large contingent of Knicks and Nets fans have jerseys or hats and Rangers, Islanders, and Devils fans sport their teams' colors too. It doesn't really matter what you own, as long as it's something. Not sporting that team gear gives

FAN TIP

Keep the flags, bumper stickers, personalized license plates, stickers, and other car decorations to a minimum. There is such a thing as overkill.

others the impression that you're either embarrassed to declare your fandom (which could understandably be true if you're a Mets, Jets, or Islanders fan) or that you're not dedicated—and therefore not a real New York sports fan. You give the appearance that you're either a closet fan, only willing to express your allegiance behind closed doors when no one is looking, or worse, a fair-weather fan. While that might not be true, it's what you're putting out there.

A simple $10 hat purchased outside the Meadowlands, Madison Square Garden, Yankee Stadium, Citi Field, the Prudential Center, or Nassau Coliseum can eliminate that problem. Ten dollars is not an unrealistic investment, no matter how bad the market or your finances are at the time. A hat is one of the easiest, cheapest alternatives to satisfying this rule, and the most common piece of paraphernalia used to show support when attending a game.

Wearing a hat isn't mandatory, but it is necessary to wear at least one piece of paraphernalia with your team's logo on it to the stadium.

things
GIANTS FANS
hate

MIRACLES OF THE MEADOWLANDS
It might be the single biggest blunder in NFL history. Plus, it was Herm Edwards who scooped Joe Pisarcik's fumble and raced toward the end zone.

RULE #10

DON'T BE THE BELICHICK OF NEW YORK SPORTS. NEVER WEAR ANYTHING FROM YOUR RIVAL

It doesn't matter if you like the Red Sox, a real Yankees fan would never wear anything with that B emblazoned on it. Heck,

Fish Tales

After the fact, WFAN producer and board-op Eddie Acosta admitted he should have known better. As a die-hard Yankees fan he should have never worn that 2003 Florida Marlins World Series Champions T-shirt into a sports-obsessed place like the FAN newsroom. In fact, he should never have worn it anywhere. After all, it is a blatant violation of a rule. The Marlins beat the Yankees in the '03 World Series, qualifying them as a bona-fide rival.

Eddie wore the shirt because he had a bet with midday co-host Evan Roberts that the Marlins would win more games in the '09 season than the Kansas City Royals. The Marlins were comfortably ahead in early July when Eddie pulled the T-shirt out of his closet (he had received it as a gag from his cousin, a Marlins fan, after the '03 series). Eddie thought it would be a good way to rub in the fact that he was going to win the bet. It was only later that he would call it an error in judgment.

Violation of Rule #10: The Marlins, who play in the same division as the Mets in the National League East, are not usually considered the Yankees' rivals. The teams have rarely faced each other since the Marlins' inception in 1993. But 2003 was different. That season, the Marlins ended the Yankees' championship dreams. Florida pitcher Josh Beckett shut them down—and then celebrated on their field. That's a memory that can never be erased. And that's what Eddie should have thought about when he put on that shirt.

they wouldn't even go near it. And if they did, the scene would probably look something like Lardass after the pie-eating contest in *Stand By Me*: a real ugly pukefest.

There is no doubt that fandom trumps style any day of the week. A Giants fan wearing an Eagles hat because you like the logo or the colors is not a valid excuse—not even close. Find something else that's green and white. For god's sake, buy a Michigan State hat if you have to. Under no circumstances is it kosher for you to go with the gear of a rival team. Besides, last we checked, nobody had a monopoly on team colors and you don't want to embarrass yourself.

Embarrassment isn't the only reason it is taboo to wear your rival's gear. It is also disrespectful to your fellow fans and the team you support. Think about it: it goes against everything that makes you a fan in the first place.

There is one exception to this rule: if it is a consequence of losing a bet. Fair is fair—you have to remain true to your word. You would expect the victor's word to be honored if the result was reversed. Just make sure once your time is up and the debt paid, you get that infernal apparel out of your house. After all, it can only soil the rest of your wardrobe.

The same concept applies if someone gives you paraphernalia from your rival team as a gift. Give it away, throw it out, burn it! Consider it a pox on your house. Just make sure it's out of your possession as soon as possible or hidden deep in a closet.

To those real fans out there, your team's rivals should be easy to identify. Still, each franchise has a long history. It's incumbent upon you, as a real fan, to have a long memory.

Mets Fans: Don't you dare wear anything from the Yankees, Phillies, Braves, or even Marlins. The first three are givens; the Marlins are on the list as a divisional opponent that has killed the Mets late in several seasons. To add insult to injury, they have enjoyed as many world championships in their first decade of existence as the Mets have accumulated in 41 years. The fellow NL East Washington Nationals aren't on the ban list because, frankly, they have yet to prove capable of playing major league-caliber baseball.

Yankees Fans: This shouldn't even be a question. Nothing Red Sox, Mets, Orioles, or Rays should ever be worn, purchased, or collected. Period. The Red Sox and Mets are givens; they are by far the Yankees' two biggest rivals. The Orioles and Rays are borderline. The Yankees and Orioles have had a sporadic rivalry over the years. Plus, the Yankees–O's will always have the

---

FAN TIP

Not only should you never wear or own any gear from rival teams, but you should also keep it out of your home, office, or car.

Armando Benitez–Tino Martinez beanball brawl and the Jeffrey Mayer play. In Baltimore, the Yankees certainly are considered hated rivals. That alone is enough to get O's banned from any Yankees fans' closet. And despite there being very little on-field competition between the Yanks and Rays, they do share the same spring training city and play in the same division.

Knicks Fans: It wouldn't be right to have anything from the Celtics, Nets, Heat, or anything old-school Bulls. The Celtics rivalry goes way back. And the Nets are right across the river. The Knicks played physical and heated series against the Bulls and Heat during the Patrick Ewing Era. Also, anything with Reggie Miller or Michael Jordan's name on it shouldn't even be given away. It should be trashed. Or burned. Or worse. Old rivalries don't die hard. Some even mature with age.

Nets Fans: Stay away from anything Knicks and Celtics. Nets fans have long held a strong hatred for the organization on the other side of the river. Those Knicks always seem to get preferential treatment. The Nets and Celtics may not be much of a rivalry today, but they did have some tough series during the Kidd years and they play in the same division.

Rangers Fans: Possessing Devils, Islanders, Flyers, or Penguins paraphernalia is forbidden. The four divisional opponents are equally disliked. As for banned players, no one should support Mario Lemieux. He and the Rangers have quite a long history,

things
METS FANS
love

TOM SEAVER
He was called "Tom Terrific" and "the Franchise." What else do you need to know?

FAN TIP

Going straight to a game from work is no excuse to not represent.
Keep your team's cap at the office, or in your briefcase or bag.

and not a pretty one at that. Lemieux had the five-goal game.
And don't forget when Adam Graves broke his wrist in the 1992
Patrick Division Finals either.

Islanders Fans: For Islanders fans, it basically starts and ends
with the Rangers. The Devils, Flyers, and Penguins are rivals
as divisional opponents. But since the only rivalry that really
matters is the Rangers, possessing anything of their New York
counterparts would be unbelievably uncivilized and inexcusable.

Devils Fans: Same goes here too. Starting to sense a theme?
The Rangers and Devils rivalry is strongest because of the
number of times they've met in big playoff series. The Flyers,
Islanders, and Penguins round out the divisional opponents that
get the ban from Devils fans.

Jets Fans: The Dolphins, Patriots, Giants, Raiders, and Colts
are banned. Period. The Giants because of jealousy, the Dolphins
because of history, and the Pats because the two franchises
have stolen players and coaches from each other for over a
decade. The Jets have also played too many important games
over the years against the Colts—who used to be in the AFC East,
remember—and Raiders to rock anything with their logo.

Giants Fans: The Eagles, Cowboys, Redskins, Jets, and even
the 49ers make this do-not-wear list. Every team in the highly
competitive NFC East is a threat, and thus a foe. Giants fans hate
them all (or if you don't, you should). The Jets are the local rival
and the 49ers have been a constant playoff opponent over the
years. And don't forget, the way the Giants blew the 2003 playoff
game in San Francisco was special—in a bad way.

RULE #11

WEAR YOUR TEAM'S LOGO TO THE GAME

If you don't satisfy Rule #9, acquiescing to this is going to be impossible. And even though wearing something to the game to support your team is relatively easy to fulfill, some patrons fail to oblige.

For a real fan, it's absolutely necessary. Fitting the part means making your allegiance visibly noticeable, even in opposing stadiums. Runners don't work out in jeans and lawyers don't go to work in bathing suits. So why would a fan go to a game in street clothes? You go in team gear because it means something. It declares you allegiance. There are no exceptions. Even if you're a working stiff coming straight from the office, this rule should be followed. Throw a hat, shirt, wristband, jersey, or something in the briefcase. Or buy one at the stadium, where you can't take two steps without crossing the path of a vendor.

RULE #12

DON'T WEAR A RANDOM JERSEY TO THE GAME

Over the past several years, jersey wearing has become more a part of the everyday wardrobe. Fans have increasingly started to wear jerseys from any sport to any game. It's absolutely ludicrous. Enough is enough. There must be jersey-wearing etiquette. You just can't go around wearing any jersey at any time—unless you desperately need the attention and you want to look incredibly foolish.

For everything, there is a time and place. Nobody wears a sombrero when they're going to play softball or takes a top hat to work (unless they're magicians). So why would you wear an Oakland Raiders jersey to a Giants-Redskins game? The

Raiders have no connection to the game or either team. It's definitely one of those *things that make you go hmmmmm*. It makes you wonder what the heck was going through that individual's head when he was getting dressed in the morning.

Even more perplexing and ridiculous is when someone elects to wear a jersey for a team in a completely different sport. Do you want to be the guy wearing a Kobe Bryant jersey at a Devils–Islanders game? Of course not. Not only do you seem like a blowhard, but you also appear confused and disoriented. What, did you get lost on your way to the Staples Center?

things
JETS FANS
hate

PLAYING IN OAKLAND
Have the Raiders ever made the trip east?

In these cases, you wonder what the possible logical explanation could be for such lunacy. But, really, there isn't one...other than the person is an idiot. Or he got dressed in the dark and grabbed the first item in his closet.

What does fly, however, is a Devils jersey if you find yourself at an Islanders-Rangers game. Or if you're a Jets fan, sport your jersey at a Bills-Patriots game. At least it's the right sport and a rival of the teams on the ice and field. It's openly showing your allegiance, loyalty, and support for a rival of the teams that are playing. That's respectable and not completely random. As long as you stick with your true allegiance, you should be good to go—provided that you can recognize what sport you're watching!

Fashion dos and don'ts are a little different for the sports fan than they are in women's magazines. Here's a crib sheet on the basic rules for stadium attire:

Appropriate
Teams Playing
Wearing something from either of the two teams on the field, court, or ice makes the most sense. The best way to showcase your allegiance, aside from cheering, is to wear something with your team's logo on it to the game.

A Player No Longer on the Team
A jersey or shirt of someone no longer on the team is in most cases fine. But always bear in mind that what's more important than the name on the back is the name on the front. Remember Rule #3, root for the uniform, not the player. Besides, with the

The Collection
To some, collecting memorabilia is a hobby. To Larry Piem, it's a passion.

Let's just say Larry has Rule #9 well covered. He doesn't just have one piece of paraphernalia for his teams, he meets the mandate several thousand times over. Larry's West Chester, N.Y., home is filled with different pieces he's collected over the years. Just to look at every piece would take hours. Bookcase after bookcase is jam-packed with all kinds of goodies that would make any fan salivate.

Many of the pieces are of Larry's two favorite teams, the Yankees and Jets. Larry, like the thousands of other sports memorabilia collectors out there, scavenges for all different kinds of things, but they're a little extra special if they're something from one of his teams.

Included among his booty is everything from scorecards, programs, baseballs, and game-worn uniforms to stadium replicas and bobbleheads. While some of the pieces are very valuable, Larry's most prized possession is something he purchased for $1. It is a program that he bought at the 1978 one-game playoff between the Yankees and Red Sox. That's right—the Bucky "F—in'" Dent game. The program has now been signed by a half-dozen players on that Yankees team, including Graig Nettles, Willie Randolph, Goose Gossage, and Chris Chambliss. It's an incredible piece of history, made even more special because of Larry's love for the Yankees, and it completes quite an impressive collection.

Wardrobe Malfunction

I waited, waited, and waited to buy a Rangers jersey. I was searching for exactly the right moment for the right player on my first-ever hockey sweater. I thought I had found him, too, when I finally, in fall 1991, pulled the trigger on a No. 9 Bernie Nicholls jersey. It was perfect—except that it never really made it out of my closet.

On October 4, just about one week after the jersey arrived, the star center was traded. This was not your average, run-of-the-mill trade. Nicholls was a substantial player at the time, someone who once scored a remarkable 70 goals in a season. The player in return?: some guy named Mark Messier. The Savior. The Messier move had been rumored for some time, but never was it linked to Nicholls. Unfortunately, he was in it. And I haven't purchased another Rangers jersey since. I'm waiting for that right moment again. —JR

frequency of player movement in today's world, it's hard to stay current. It often requires a significant financial investment that some are unable to make.

A Rival of Your Team's Opponent
Wearing the jersey of a rival team to a game of either of the two teams on the field, court, or ice is acceptable. Just bear in mind that in some places it's safer to do this than in others. We don't recommend it at a football game in Philadelphia, Oakland, or Buffalo, for instance. At those venues, such behavior puts your life in jeopardy.

Most Novelty Jerseys
It's always funny to see a Cleveland Indians jersey with Vaughn on the back, a Cameron Frye Red Wings sweater, or a Henry Rowengartner Cubs jersey. We'll even let you slide with something like a gag jersey with the name High and the numeral 5 below it. Trust us, these jerseys are out there.

Inappropriate

Personalized Jerseys
Get a life. Benigno never played for the Jets. Never will, either.
The only way you can get away with it is if there happens to be
another guy on the team with the same last name as yours.

Random Teams
Attending a Devils-Islanders game in a Ducks jersey makes no
sense. If you do it, you're an attention-starved loser.

The Wrong Sport
Why would anyone wear a football jersey to a baseball game? It's
like showing up to your softball game in a wetsuit.

A Hated Former Player
A Devils fan in his right mind would never wear a Scott Gomez
jersey—even if it is the only jersey in the closet. Gomez went to
the dark side: the Rangers. That will never be forgotten by Devils
fans. No jersey is worse to wear to a Devils game than a Gomez
jersey.

RULE #13

CHOOSE YOUR JERSEY CAREFULLY

A lot goes into selecting which player's jersey to purchase. Make
the wrong choice and you might never take it out of the closet.
That player could get traded, hold out, or demand a trade the
very next day, leaving you unwilling (and by rule, unable) to ever
wear it proudly.

Trust us, it's happened before and will happen again. Jason
Siet is a perfect example. A die-hard Mets fan, he wanted to
purchase a jersey that was both unique and real. So he shelled
out a substantial amount of money and purchased an authentic
Ty Wigginton jersey for $225. He even shelled out extra because

The New Jerseys

According to our own expert observations, what were the most common jerseys of choice in 2009?

Yankees: The more thing change, the more they stay the same. Derek Jeter's No. 2 is a stadium staple. John Chamberlain, Mark Teixeira, A.J. Burnett, and CC Sabathia jerseys are some of the fresher options, but Jeter is still the face of the franchise.

Mets: Johan Santana's No. 57. Can you go wrong with the best pitcher in baseball? Carlos Beltran, David Wright, and Jose Reyes also received solid support. And for good reason. They've all proven themselves with the team.

Jets: He may not be on the field, but retired wide receiver Wayne Chrebet's No. 80 is still the most popular jersey in the stands (particularly since those hastily purchased Brett Favre jerseys have been placed in storage). That's not saying a lot for the franchise. Hopefully Sanchez can soon overtake him.

Giants: Eli Manning. The quarterback often gets the credit for a Super Bowl victory. Especially young QBs with a bright future.

Rangers: Mark Messier and Brian Leetch. Oh, those glory days. The 21st century hasn't been too kind to the Rangers, which is why you're more likely to see the fans do it old school.

Islanders: Rick DiPietro. Not many players sign 15-year contracts. At least Islanders fans know he has a future with the team. You can't say that about too many other players. 2009 No. 1 overall pick John Tavares is also a strong candidate.

Devils: Martin Brodeur. One of the all-time greats. He's an easy choice for both die-hard and fringe fans.

Knicks: Nate Robinson. Winning the dunk contest sells a lot of jerseys, even for bench players. Plus, with the Knicks personnel on the floor, it was slim pickings. (This should change in 2010.)

Nets: Jason Kidd. The most popular player on the best teams in franchise history. The Nets have not come anywhere close to matching their previous success with Kidd. Nobody forgets that.

METS FANS love things

THE HOME RUN APPLE

So beloved that a new, bigger version sits in the outfield at Citi Field. A Mets home run wouldn't be the same without it.

of the extra letters in the last name. But Jason liked Wigginton because he was a tough, scrappy player who was fairly young. He thought he was going to be with the Mets for a very long time.

The problem with this thinking was that Wigginton was an average player without an assured long-term future with the club. Not surprisingly, soon enough, Wigginton was gone several months later, moved to Pittsburgh in a package for pitcher Kris Benson. The jersey hasn't come out of Jason's closet since. He hasn't purchased another real jersey either, only replicas. Even then, it's only one of the staples, the stars. Johan Santana, David Wright, and Mike Piazza.

Sure, Wigginton could have remained on the Mets as a utility player for the next decade, but longevity on a single team for players like him are uncommon. That's why it's imperative to do your due diligence before making a purchase—especially for something as costly as a team jersey. It's like going to buy a television or car: you don't buy on impulse. Of course, nothing is foolproof.

Buyer Beware

Purchasing a jersey can be a tricky proposition. It's rather easy to make the wrong decision. After all, you can wake up the next morning and that player could be on his way out of town. That decision is obviously not in your hands unless you happen to be the GM (in which case you're not spending money on team apparel anyway). So do some research and take these factors into consideration to avoid making a poor investment.

Find a Player Who Has Already Proven Himself with the Team
This immediately eliminates free-agent signings and draft picks—and for good reason. History dictates that a rather large percentage of trumpeted acquisitions turn out to be busts. (This is especially true of any Jets draft pick.) Remember Blair Thomas? What about Robbie Alomar? Carl Pavano? Wade Redding? Jumping the gun most often leaves you with a jersey that is more likely destined to reach the garbage than be worn.

Staying Power
You want the jersey to be relevant for as long as possible. When Derek Jeter signed his 10-year, $189-million deal in 2001, it was a pretty good bet he was going to be with the Yankees for a while. That's key. You must make sure that the player has a bright future and long-term contract. Getting a Tom Glavine Mets jersey would have been a foolish investment. He joined the Mets on a three-year contract in the tail end of his career. He was destined for just a few years with the team. Even though Glavine actually stayed for four years, they weren't overly successful. Not to mention that his Mets career ended with one of his worst performances, when the Mets needed to win on the final day of the '07 season.

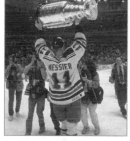

**things
DEVILS FANS
hate**

**MARK MESSIER'S
GUARANTEE**
The only thing worse than Messier guaranteeing a Game 6 victory was him being right.

things
YANKEES FANS
hate

BILL MAZEROSKI
The 1960 World Series ended on
a long ball from a player known
almost exclusively for his defense: a
hard pill to swallow.

Be Unique
Think outside the box if possible.
Be different and distinguish
yourself from the phonies who
don't know any better. Try to get
a jersey that is not the generic,
popular choice of the fan who
doesn't know any better. Everyone
has a Jeter jersey. Mariano Rivera,
Jorge Posada...now those are fairly
unique yet cool choices.

Be Financially Prudent if Needed
Nobody cares if you have an
authentic, officially licensed jersey,
which can really set you back.
The replicas do the job just fine.
Each team's fan base needs to
take special consideration before
slecting a jersey.

Jets fans: be especially wary of high draft picks. Blair
Thomas, Johnny Lam Jones, Dave Cadigan, Jeff Lageman, Kyle
Brady, and Dewayne Robertson are just a few of the ignominious
names over recent years. Clearly, history is not on your side.

Mets fans: Free-agent signings are your Achilles' heel. Vince
Coleman, Kevin Appier, Bobby Bonilla, Roberto Alomar, and Mo
Vaughn are among those who highlight the list of high-profile
signings who grossly underachieved.

Yankees fans: Don't you dare dip into the farm system. Most
of the team's prospects are traded before they ever make it to
the big leagues.

Rangers fans: Former Devils are never as good when
they cross the river. Bobby Holik and Scott Gomez are the
evidence.

I Dos and Don'ts, Part One

Eric Baumgarten is such a die-hard Rangers fan that he felt compelled to incorporate the team into his wedding. Wearing one of his jerseys was out of the question (there would have been no wedding had he insisted on this being the case). So he did the next best thing. Eric wore a Rangers-themed yarmulke during the ceremony. That's dedication! Even better, it was a gift from his wife—in fact, it was the first gift she gave to him. (Talk about knowing the best way to a real New York sports fan's heart.) Amazingly, she bought the yarmulke for him at a deli. It might be fair to say his wife is now married to the Rangers too.

Devils fans: Make sure you get a long-term commitment. Management has been very careful in selecting which players will have a long run in New Jersey.

Islanders fans: Supposed big-name players acquired via trade have not worked out often. Stay away from their jerseys or you might end up very disappointed.

RULE #14

DON'T GO OVERBOARD

It's one thing to represent your team. It's another to look like a walking billboard. That's the result if you're wearing a Yankees hat, jersey, shorts, socks, underwear, and wristbands. You look more ridiculous than Billy Ho.

There needs to be some kind of limit. Let's set it at two items. Anything more is overload and it will make you look like the middle-aged guy who still lives with his mother. Also, lay off the team-endorsed accessories. Giants wristbands don't need to be worn to games (or any other time, for that matter).

PART FIVE

WATCH IT

RULE #15

DON'T MISS MANY, IF ANY, GAMES

The Jets and Giants each have 16 games on their regular-season schedule. A National Football League game lasts approximately 3½ hours. So for every regular season there is a total 56 hour commitment necessary to watch or listen to every second of every game—plus some possible postseason action, if you're lucky. That's no Herculean time commitment, especially for die-hard New York sports fans like us. It's also a big reason why football is the most popular and successful sport in the country.

In every NBA and NHL regular season there are 82 games at an estimated 2½ hours apiece. The entire season is an 82-day, 205-hour commitment for the Knicks, Nets, Rangers, Islanders, or Devils. That might not seem like a lot, but it is more than most can handle. Eighty-two days is close to three full months. And 205 hours is 8½ straight days. Imagine watching games without any interruptions or sleep for more than a week straight. Pretty intense.

Major League Baseball is even more ridiculous. There are 162 regular-season games at an estimated three hours per clip. To watch or listen to an entire season would require more than

FAN TIP

Don't plan a wedding on a Sunday from September to February. You're just asking for trouble.

five months and 486 hours, which is the equivalent of spending more than 20 straight days of 24/7 baseball. That's a ton. Considered thusly, rooting for the Mets or Yankees is more than twice the commitment needed to support every second of the Knicks, Nets, Rangers, Islanders, or Devils' seasons, and more than eight times the commitment for an NFL season.

Watching or listening to every game played by any of those teams would require that your life be centered around the team. As it is, most New York sports fans have a daily or weekly routine that accomodates watching or listening to games. Committing to every game is way too much time for most sane humans. In fact, we find it unlikely there are many, if any, fans who have watched every pitch during an entire 162-game season. If there are, we haven't found them yet—probably because they have not left their houses in years.

Watching or listening to every game, every minute, and every play of an entire baseball, basketball, or hockey season is out of the question for most of us. (Though not all. See sidebar on Miriam from Forest Hills.) Even for a dedicated New York sports fan, it's a hefty time investment to contemplate. Some real fans may watch or listen to most of their team's games, say 90 percent, but there are times when it's just not possible. Believe it or not, there are other things in life aside from your rooting interest.

An entire NFL season is a different story. While it's still unlikely to catch every single minute, play, and snap, it is a much more realistic goal—even if most fans do have lives, kids, family affairs, or other interests and commitments that consume some of their Sundays. Even the most dedicated fans are likely to miss a game or two.

To mandate watching or listening to an entire season in any sport is a bit too ambitious. We're just going to set a minimum requirement for the true New York sports fan in each of the four major sports. For a die-hard, these requirements are a cinch; you can do it in your sleep. The numbers don't include the time that the degenerate New York sports fans also put into watching golf, soccer, tennis, auto racing, UFC, boxing, or whatever else sparks their interest.

Due to the unique nature of each sport, the requirements differ. The common denominator, of course, is that it's imperative not to miss too many games. What constitutes too many games is relative to the length of each season. Missing four Jets games is a lot more costly than missing four Mets games. That why we mandate watching or listening to at least part of 65 percent of Mets and Yankees games, 75 percent of Knicks and Nets games, and 75 percent of Rangers, Islanders, and Devils games. For football, where the smallest number of game commitments is required, that ratio is somewhere around 85 percent.

The All-82er

Miriam from Forest Hills, the name she goes by when she calls into WFAN, might be blind, but she doesn't miss a beat when it comes to her Islanders. A fan since their inception, Miriam covers the game requirement rather easily. In fact, she blows it away, rarely ever missing a radio broadcast for her favorite team.

How many games does Miriam hear each season? Oh, just a measly all 82. And the playoffs? Every last one of them.

She admits that she did miss one regular-season game a few years back because she "had something else to do." She's about as pure and real as a fan can be. She puts the time and emotional investment into every Islanders game and season, no matter how bad the team might be that particular year. It doesn't matter whether they are stuck in the cellar or in the midst of a playoff run, Miriam is there, by her radio, listening to her beloved Islanders.

Why does she do it? Why does she put herself through all of the terrible seasons, bad losses, and dumbfounding trades? Why does she subject herself to such cruelty? "Because it's fun," she said. It's not cruel at all for a fan like Miriam. She enjoys every last second because she is a true New York sports fan.

Viewing or Listening Requirements
(not including postseason play)

Mets and Yankees Fans
Season: 162 games
Requirement: 105 games

Jets and Giants Fans
Season: 16 games
Requirements: 14 games

Knicks and Nets Fans
Season: 82 games
Requirement: 62 games

Rangers, Devils, and Islanders fans:
Season: 82 games
Requirement: 62 games

Clearly, no matter the sport, real New York sports fans must make a significant commitment to their teams. That means you need to have SNY, the YES Network, or MSG set as favorites. There is no way you can come close to fulfilling your obligations without them or the team's radio partners. So set that remote or radio dial.

There are several reasons why it's necessary for real New York sports fans to watch or listen to so many games. The first is that you never know when something great or classic is going to happen. You don't want to miss that once-in-a-lifetime moment.

One of those moments was on June 13, 2009, in what looked to be just another run-of-the-mill Subway Series game between the Mets and Yankees. Except that's when the unthinkable happened. Alex Rodriguez hits a pop-up to second base with two outs and two men on in the ninth inning at Citi Field. Mets second baseman Luis Castillo sets up for the routine catch on the pop-up but the ball hits the heel of his glove, both runners score, and the Yankees win the game, 9–8.

The play will likely be the most memorable regular season Subway Series moment of all time. It was something that you may never see again in your lifetime—a dropped popup with two outs in the ninth inning to lose a game. It's not often, if ever, that a Little League miscue like that occurs in a major league game. You might not believe it if you hadn't seen it.

Of course, if you happened to miss the Friday night game, surely you saw the replay 1,000 times on the local news, *SportsNight*, *SportsCenter*, and so on. You probably read everything about it in the papers too, and heard it broken down by fans and commentators on the radio. But it's still not the same as seeing it live.

That's because it is one of the most infamous plays in Mets history and yet still one that Mets fans would have wanted to see live. For those who didn't, their first reaction was likely, *I can't believe I missed it*, even though it was a painful outcome—arguably as bad a regular-season loss as there has been in team history. And Yankees fans also wanted to be tuned in so they could say they saw the ridiculous drop.

Real New York sports fans want to be there for it all, the good and the bad. They watch and digest classic moments like when Castillo dropped the ball, and they're there when, one day, they are on the other side of the error. Or when a Mets pitcher actually throws the franchise's first no-hitter. These are moments you

things METS FANS love

MR. MET
His big head doesn't make him any less likable.

Rare Misses

I never miss Jets games. Actually, I really never miss any football games. Especially playoff football. I've seen every Jets games since '02, and still counting. The last game I missed was in 2002, when they eventually would make the playoffs. It was a late-afternoon game and I was due at a wedding. There was no way out of it. If there had been, I would have taken it.

It was funny because everyone at the time knew who I was and kept coming up to me and giving me scores of the game. Luckily, the team didn't need me. Chad Pennington threw four touchdown passes in the victory. It's the only Jets game that I've missed since my college days in the '70s when I was in Indiana. (I wasn't able to watch the Jets games there; every week we got the Bengals and the Bears.)

But it's not just Jets games I watch. It's the playoffs too—all the playoffs. In January '93, my now-wife and I were dating, and she was over at my house for the weekend. I was watching this playoff game, Buffalo and Houston. It was 35-3 Oilers early in the third. I figured it was over, so I decided to go take care of business. I wasn't going to miss anything. I came back later, put the game back on, and it was 38-35 Bills. **What, are you kidding me?** I can't believe I missed it; they were all the way back in the game.

From that point on I vowed I would never, ever do anything like that again during an NFL playoff game. That can't happen. Never again. And I have held true to my word. I won't miss any playoff game, whether the Jets are playing or not. —JB

don't want to miss. Never knowing when those moments are going to come, the key is to catch as many of them as you can.

New York sports fans also watch the bulk of the games to stay in tune with what's going on with their teams. If you miss several games, upon your return you feel like you've missed so much. You don't know the intricacies of what is going on with the team— who is struggling, who is hot, who is injured. You feel lost. You feel as if you missed a crucial piece of the season-long journey. If you were out of the country and missed the Castillo game, you missed a turning point in the Mets' season. You were not there when they had to overcome certain very difficult obstacles, because losing a game in that fashion is definitely not easy.

But even if they missed it, real New York sports fans return and watch, hoping they won't miss the next once-in-a-lifetime moment or game.

RULE #16

NEVER MISS A PLAYOFF GAME

When the Rangers lost to the Flyers in the '97 Eastern Conference Finals, the natural assumption was that they would be back the next year fighting for a Stanley Cup. After all, the Rangers had just made their 18th playoff appearance in 20 years. Making the playoffs seemed like a birthright. Unfortunately, contrary to what some Rangers or Yankees fans think, making the playoffs is not an inalienable right. Not every team qualifies for the postseason (although it seems like it sometimes, when more than half the teams do in the NHL and NBA).

Knicks fans were spoiled for a long time. They watched their team make the playoffs in 14 straight seasons during the Patrick Ewing Era. After the long stretch of impressive success—though sans an NBA title—they failed to make the postseason a single time from 2002 to 2009. It just goes to show, you never known when the magic carpet ride is going to end. Nobody would have guessed that the Jets would go decades without making it back to the Super Bowl following their Super Bowl III triumph. Or that the Islanders' last Stanley Cup would be in 1983 after winning their fourth straight.

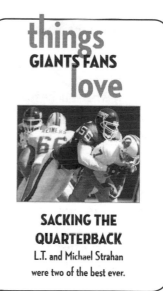

things
GIANTS FANS
love

SACKING THE QUARTERBACK
L.T. and Michael Strahan were two of the best ever.

I Dos and Don'ts, Part Two

If you want to have your wedding remembered forever, have it on a football Sunday. The only problem then is that it's not necessarily going to be remembered for the beautiful ceremony or top-notch lamb chops. It will go down in infamy as the wedding that occurred during the Jets game.

To many of those who attended Scott and Melissa Epstein's wedding on October 24, 2004, the most lasting memory is the back bar at Brooklake Country Club. There, crowded around televisions showing the Jets-Patriots game, was a group of wedding refugees rooting on Gang Green. Both teams had entered that Week 7 contest with perfect 5-0 records. Even Giants fans wanted to see that one.

The most perplexing part of it all is that the groom is a die-hard Jets fan. Unfortunately, he allowed what at the time was his soon-to-be-bride to select the date knowing full well the Jets would almost certainly be playing that afternoon. You see, Melissa wanted a fall wedding with outdoor pictures, and she got it because Scott was not willing to put his foot down. (Though in his defense, they chose the date before Scott knew the Jets would be playing the defending champion Patriots.)

It just goes to show the power of the women. They not only force and pressure you into marriage, but they also sometimes get you to do it on a football Sunday. What can't they do?

The moral of the story is, enjoy it when you can. You never know when success will evade you and there will be no playoff games to see or hear. Just like that, the lights can be flicked off. After all, even the Yankees went over a decade starting in the '80s and continuing into the '90s without a playoff appearance.

That's why you should cherish your team's playoff games whenever possible. Never—barring limited extenuating circumstances—miss the opportunity to watch a playoff game. TiVo it if you have to, but there is nothing like the atmosphere and intensity of a playoff game. Rearrange your schedule if possible. And if you can wriggle out of that wedding, baptism, bar or bat mitzvah, or anniversary party, do it.

You never know when the next classic game or moment is going to occur, and if it's your team in the playoffs you certainly don't want to miss when it happens. It's bad enough when you miss that once-in-a-lifetime moment in the regular season. Not being there for it in the postseason is an incredibly tough pill to swallow.

RULE #17

STICK WITH IT UNTIL THE END

The Mets are playing a late-afternoon game against the Dodgers, the Rangers are hosting the Devils that night, and a new season of *Curb Your Enthusiasm* is beginning. Options, options, options. So much to watch, so little time. Better have the remote handy.

In these types of situations, you're going to jump around. You *have* to jump around. You can't watch it all. Here's our suggestion: tape *Curb* or whatever other television program you're attached to and watch those games live. If that is not an option, at least make sure that you're back for the final few innings or minutes of each game.

End-game situations are crucial. It's when most of the big plays happen. A 15-foot jump shot Patrick Ewing hit in the second quarter pales in comparison to the one he made in the final seconds. Alex Rodriguez's third-inning at-bat won't be dissected the same way as his final one, either. It is the end of the game when heroes and goats are born.

things YANKEES FANS love

PERFECT GAMES
They've had four, including the only thrown in World Series history, by Don Larsen.

Leaving the game early to beat traffic early is a huge rule violation. Think of it this way: if you stay for the whole game, you'll not only see your team's full performance, but you could also be the last people in the parking lot.

In no sport is this more true than in basketball, when the first half or the three quarters often proves completely meaningless. In a large majority of basketball games, more so than any other sport, the final result is contingent on who plays best the final five minutes.

So no matter what and especially if the game is close, be there for the final inning, quarter, or period. And in the final inning or minute (depending on your sport, of course) put the remote down completely. Real New York fans wouldn't want to miss a thing.

There are times to work the clicker hard and times to have it glued to the table. Here are some basic guidelines to help you determine when to change the channel:

Do flip during commercials.
For the most part, unless we're talking about the Super Bowl, ads aren't worth catching. Plus, there are so many other quality options available, many times including other games. People purchase the sports packages for a reason. They want to pop in and out of games. A requirement for that is flipping channels.

Don't flip during a playoff game
At this crucial juncture in a team's season, the channel should not even change during commercials. The tide can turn in a game quickly, and you could miss that play while you're catching that scene from *Trading Places* on the next channel. You don't want that. Next thing you know, you've missed the greatest comeback in team history and you're kicking yourself stupid.

Don't flip during the course of NFL action.
You wait, wait, and wait some more for something big to happen. Then boom, it finally does. You never know which play is going to be the big one if you weren't flipping. The season is too short to miss it.

Do flip during a blowout.
Finally a chance to check out some of the other quality programming available from those 1,000 channels, right? If there is a better option available, change the channel. No need to watch the end of a massacre.

Do flip if you have a conflict of interest.
Sports seasons overlap, leaving plenty conflicts of interest for fans of multiple sports. The Knicks and Rangers games are often played at the same time. And the Yankees' and Mets' seasons sometimes extend into October or even November, when the NBA and NHL are in full swing.

Do flip early in games.
It's permissable to surf at the beginning of games, as long as it's not an NFL contest. Just make sure you're back for the late-game play. After all, that's when all the crucial, memorable moments happen.

Don't flip for American Idol *or any other reality show.*
Have some standards! Get a hold of yourself! Singing and dancing aren't normally the other pastimes for die-hard sports fans.

PART SIX

IN THE HOUSE

RULE #18

ATTEND AT LEAST ONE GAME EACH SEASON

The comforts of the couch are nice but, once in a while, there is nothing more satisfying than smelling the fresh air, grass, or ice. The excitement of hearing the pop of the mitt from a 90-plus mile-per-hour fastball, the crack of the bat, the roar of the crowd after a crushing hit or dunk, or the ding of the puck slamming off the crossbar and out of harm's way can't be replicated from the Barcalounger. The sights and sounds of actually being in the stadium or arena are irreplaceable.

Hey, we love lounging on the couch, pants unbuttoned after a large meal, relaxing with our wife beside us just as much as the next guy. Sometimes, though, it's good to get out and alter the routine, to join 20,000 to 80,000 of our closest friends in rooting on our favorite team.

So we do it with a smile. We get off our lazy asses and head to the ballpark or the arena at least once a year. You should do it too. It's refreshing cathartic even. All the suppressed anger or joy you've built while sitting in front of the TV during the season can finally be released. At the game, you can yell or scream as loud as you want without your spouse thinking

Getting to the stadium at least once a season is required. Body paint, on the other hand, is optional.

you're a demented lunatic. In fact, you'll just blend in with everyone else.

You can also enjoy a much different viewpoint than the one you get at home, where you're at the mercy of the network cameras. The TV cameras determine what you will and will not see. At the actual event, the scope is bigger. All the peripheral action is at your disposal. Everything from the game action to the cheerleaders to the vendors to your fellow fans in the stands. You have a full view of the whole enchilada. It's a unique, beautiful thing, and a different first-hand perspective that every New York sports fan should enjoy at least once each season.

The upper deck at the Meadowlands allows you to be on top of the play and watch everything develop. The blocking, the patterns, the defensive schemes, are all right there for you to decode. You can see when the quarterback fails to spot a wide-open receiver or when the running back slips coming out of the backfield. A lower-level end-zone seat gives you a close-up to the action when it approaches your half of the field. You can determine whether the running back hits his hole or chooses the wrong lane, whether the defender should have made the tackle or failed to get off his block. Every section has its benefits, with advantages and disadvantages to each (yes, even those luxury boxes). But they all provide vastly different viewpoints than the television broadcast.

The view isn't the only reason to get to at least one game a year. There is also tailgating, fan interaction, and the amenities of the stadiums or arenas themselves, most of which will be new by the start of the 2010 seasons. (The Giants and Jets, Mets and Yankees, and Devils will all have pristine, modern facilities by the end of 2010.) That's all just gravy though. Real sports fans go for the game. More than anything, they go to see their team win. They want to experience that feeling of joy as they walk out the gates following a victory.

There is no way to reproduce the feeling of a win with thousands of people, all of whom are cheering and sharing the same goal. It's also thrilling to be amongst the enemy, hoping for a victory in unfriendly confines. Either way, leaving with a win is an invigorating feeling.

Attending home games is a bonding experience like no other. You're connecting with a huge audience. You can hang with family and friends on the couch at home all season long.

Transplant Candidate

The West Coast hasn't taken any of the Big Blue out of Seth Leibick. Despite moving from Manhattan in 2006, his Giants fandom hasn't faded one bit. In fact, it might be stronger than ever. Seth has done everything to watch his Giants in San Francisco, maybe even more than before. He has attended a handful of games each season. He found sports bars that showed the Giants games on Sunday and planned trips back home that aligned with home games.

Despite relocating, Seth has followed Rule #18. Attend at Least One Game Each Season with relative ease. He even sat in minus-24 wind chill weather in Green Bay for the 2008 NFC Championship Game. Now that's true dedication.

At least once a season, however, it's good to remember all the other people who are out there rooting for the same team. At the stadium, it's lively. This makes the action, in a way, more real. The trip is always an experience, win or lose.

Plus, by attending games, you contribute to helping your team win. Being at the stadium and voicing your support for the team is a contribution. You're doing your part. You and thousands of others bolster the players' effort with your energy and excitement. And it helps. It's why the home team has an advantage in any contest. Fans can and do make a difference in the game. As a die-hard fan of that team, you should be part of that.

Cheering lifts players' spirits and makes them put in that little bit of extra effort that could make the difference. It's all part of the reason home teams in every sport have a significantly better record than they do away. Even average teams possess winning

The Road Warrior

Want passion? Try this on for lunacy.

Ira Leiberfarb is a Jets fan. A **big** Jets fan. A season-ticket holder since the early '70s, he attends all the team's home games. So what? Well, Ira also attends all of the Jets away games—including postseason and preseason! We'll let you digest that one for a second.... Yes, including preseason. Ira attends preseason road games in which the only guys playing are ones who won't even make the CFL.

That is passion for your team—passion that's hard to find anywhere outside of New York. The last game Ira missed was a 30-3 loss in Carolina during the 2005 season. Since then, he's attended every single Jets road contest—some with his wife, others with his cousin, and—get this—plenty by himself. In about six of eight road games each season, Ira travels alone.

It all started for Ira when he took a road trip with his cousin during the 1994 season. Then it really picked up steam around the 2000 campaign. By 2004, Ira was fully committed. He would attend every Jets game he possibly could. And he did, no matter the destination. He's been to New England, Seattle, San Diego, and Miami, touching all four corners of the U.S. map. Now that's a sign of passion.

home marks. During the 2008 NFL regular season, five teams finished with 8–8 records, but none had losing records at home. In Major League Baseball, of the three teams that finished within three games of .500, all three were at least nine games over at home. In the NBA, all five teams within three games of .500 had strong home marks. The same is true for hockey. All 16 playoff teams were no lower than five games above .500. Fans definitely have something to do with this success, which is why you should be a part of it.

Being at the game exemplifies a different level of support than watching the games at home. You are supporting the team not only through your cheers but also through your wallet. It's imperative that at least once each year you get out, throw on some paraphernalia (as stated in Rule #11) and be a part of the action. If you live in the United States but out of the team's home area, try to catch your favorite team when they come closest to your town. The Yankees and Mets play at least three games in every region of the country, from the Northeast to the Southwest, which should make it possible for you to get to a stadium near you by car once each year. The Rangers, Islanders, Devils, Knicks, Nets, and Jets also play all over the country, and the Devils, Islanders, and Rangers even head north to Canada. Only Alaskans and Hawaiians should have trouble making arrangments. So check the schedule and figure out what works best for you. And don't forget, you're always welcome in New York too.

RULE #19

TAKE PUBLIC TRANSPORTATION IF POSSIBLE

Traffic is a bitch. What else can you say? The Tri-State area is densely populated, with more residents per square foot than any other area in the United States. That inevitably makes for densely packed roads anytime, not the least of which during game days.

Driving to any major sporting event in the Tri-State area is a big risk. The 10 miles from midtown Manhattan to the Meadowlands almost never takes 15 minutes. Sometimes it takes two hours. You never know when you're going to miss an inning, quarter, period, or entire half.

That's why there are other options. New York, after all, is a big city. And by virtue of its size, it has an extremely sophisticated public transportation system that can get you practically anywhere you need to go. You need to get to the Meadowlands from Manhattan early in the morning? No problem. You want to travel from Madison Square Garden to North Jersey late at night? Easy. You're trekking to the Nassau Coliseum from the city in the afternoon? You're there.

Whether it's by train or bus, New Jersey transit, the subway, PATH, or Long Island Railroad, New York sports fans can get to games without a car. In fact, it's ideal. Public transportation is almost always just minutes away. It's relatively quick, easy, cheap, reliable, and effective. Added bonus: fans can drink before and during games without any concerns about having to drive home. Talk about a win-win situation. Not to mention, it's the green alternative.

Whenever possible, take public transportation. The only exception to this rule is for you tailgaters out there. After all, some things take precedence.

RULE #20

NEVER LEAVE WHEN THE GAME IS STILL IN DOUBT

Some concepts seem so simple and obvious they should never need to be discussed. For instance, don't piss against the wind. Hopefully you figured that one out by yourself at a very young age. If not, don't shake our hands, please.

Common sense says that if you went to a sporting event to cheer on your team, there is no way you should leave with the game still in doubt. Shockingly, though, it happens all the time. Three minutes left in the game and the Giants have the ball, trailing by three. A field goal will tie and a touchdown gives them a win. But some so-called fans are heading to the exit at Giants Stadium. To do what, beat the traffic? Catch the final few minutes on the radio? Why even bother going to the game in the first place and invest three hours just to leave before a winner is determined?

It makes no sense whatsoever. None. You don't go take the SATs and leave five questions before the end of the test just to beat the rush. You've already spent three, four, five hours; what are a few extra minutes? It's like starting to mow your lawn but not finishing because you refuse to spend more than two hours doing any household task. Once the second hand hits two hours, you head inside and leave your lawn looking like Ron Artest's head after a trip to the barber. The job is clearly unfinished, yet you refuse to continue.

There is no plausible explanation for such foolishness, just as there is no way to explain why any "fan" would leave before the outcome of the game is decided. A real New York sports fan would never commit such an atrocious error. Only the phonies, fakes, and frauds would show so little interest in the final result that avoiding traffic is a higher priority.

Some might say the warped line of thinking is caused by the fast-paced New York lifestyle in which everyone is always in a

things
JETS FANS
love

RETIRED WIDE RECEIVERS
Keyshawn Johnson, Wayne Chrebet, Al Toon, and Wesley Walker remain popular.

rush. Sure, nobody wants to be stuck on a highway that feels more like a parking lot. Sitting in the massive traffic jam that inevitably follows when leaving a stadium is not fun, but that excuse doesn't fly with die-hard New York sports fans.

If you're a real fan, you come to see your favorite team win (or lose) the game. So stay until the result is in the books. In fact, some fans refuse to leave until the clock hits 00:00, even if the result appears evident well before time elapses. In laymen's terms,

Beat the Clock

David Henry has a rule of his own. He never leaves a Jets game until the clock says 00:00, no matter the weather, score, or impending traffic. There have been plenty of times when his sons, wife, daughter-in-law, and others have begged to leave in the face of the Jets' insurmountable deficits. But David was unmoved. He was not going to leave early no matter how cold, rainy, snowy, or balmy the weather. He would never risk that one time when the Jets actually completed the improbable comeback—or so he thought.

Everybody was convinced he was crazy, wasting his time and making his family suffer unnecessarily through blowouts in inclement weather. But on a Monday night in 2000, David committed the cardinal sin. He went against everything he believed in and broke his own rule for the first time in 20 years of attending Jets games. David left early—and boy, did he get punished.

With the Jets hosting the rival Miami Dolphins and the despised Dan Marino, they trailed by 23 points entering the fourth quarter. Midnight crept closer and an early wakeup call for work the following morning loomed. His wife and son begged to go; he listened. After three quarters of action, they headed home. The game was still in progress when they got there.

No big deal. All he missed was the second-largest fourth-quarter comeback in NFL history and the contest was voted the greatest game in **Monday Night Football** history. David got burned, big time. He missed the Jets' 30-point fourth quarter, which was capped by a touchdown from the most improbable of sources: offensive tackle Jumbo Elliot.

How do you get over something like that? The comeback David had waited to see for all those years from his upper-deck, 50-yard-line seat was finally happening, but with him at home. It was little consolation that David caught the game-winning, overtime field goal on television at home.

At least it was a lesson well learned. You'll never find David leaving another game until the final whistle.

they won't even leave a blowout early. They don't want to get burned and miss that one magical ending they had been waiting for all these years. Those people who leave early in close games are just asking to get burned.

That's why it's so hard to fathom spending three hours and precious money on something and then heading for the exits before it's over. Would you leave a movie five minutes before its conclusion? Some sports fans obviously justify this ridiculous behavior because you see it all the time. As real New York sports fans, though, you can't accept or condone this type of behavior. You would never even contemplate such a senseless act.

things RANGERS FANS love

MSG
The world's greatest arena for hockey (and basketball too).

Exiting a game early leaves you vulnerable to missing a classic. That's the ultimate insult. You attend a game, spend several hours and plenty of money at the stadium or arena, and then miss the greatest game and ending in franchise history? That sucks. But you have no one to blame but yourself. By the time you arrived at home, you almost certainly were amazed when you learned about the final result. And no doubt you were kicking yourself for it too.

Hope you didn't miss it

Devils vs. Hurricanes in the 2009 Playoffs
If you tried to beat the traffic with 80 seconds remaining in Game 7 of the Devils' first-round series against the Hurricanes, you missed a classic meltdown. The great Marty Brodeur surrendered two goals in the final 1:20 and the Devils' season

FAN TIP

At least once in your lifetime, sit in the upper deck at the
50-yard line to get a completely different perspective.

ended at home with a demoralizing 3–2 loss. Some may say this
was the worst loss in team history, although Stephane Matteau
might not agree.

Yankees vs. Diamondbacks in the 2001 World Series
Take your pick. If you left prior to the ninth inning of Games 4
and 5 at Yankee Stadium, you missed some serious drama. Tino
Martinez victimized Byung-Hyun Kim with a two-run homer in
the ninth inning of Game 4 to even the score. Derek Jeter ended
Game 4 in extra innings with his Mr. November act. Scott Brosius
hit a clutch ninth-inning homer in Game 5.

Mets vs. Braves in the 2000 Regular Season
The stands were half empty in this July 1 contest by the time
the Mets' offense awoke with a 10-run eighth inning against
the rival Atlanta Braves. The Mets were trailing 8–1 entering
the frame and won 11–8. Nine of the runs came with two outs
in the inning. Mike Piazza's three-run homer proved to be the
difference.

Knicks vs. Pacers in the 1995 Playoffs
Fans were headed for the exits early with the Knicks up six and
just 18.7 seconds remaining. Then the bottom fell out. The
Pacers' Reggie Miller dropped eight points in 16.4 seconds to
secure a come-from-behind 107–105 victory over the Knicks in
Game 1 of their Eastern Conference semifinals series at Madison
Square Garden. Those fans who left missed a once-in-a-lifetime
ending, capped by Miller miming "choke" to Spike Lee and the
rest of the crowd that remained in the arena.

Jets vs. Dolphins in the 2000 Regular Season
A large portion of fans had already left the stadium before one of the greatest comebacks in Jets history was completed. The Jets overcame a 27-point fourth-quarter deficit and won 40–37 in the Monday Night Miracle. The seats were mostly empty when the game ended well past midnight.

RULE #21

SIT WITH THE REAL FANS

Every section and row in a stadium has a different, unique vibe, especially in the ultimate grab bag that is New York. There are different chants, characters, agendas, and camaraderie in each. One section might be harshly critical of a specific player while the one adjacent to it offers words of encouragement. One might be calling for the coach's head, the other defending his decisions. That's the beauty of attending games in the Tri-State area. There are so many varying viewpoints and opinions among fans.

Some say timing is everything, but when attending a game, it's location, location, location. You want to be with the real fans, the ones who have an undying passion for the team and the game. In each stadium or arena, they can be found in a different area. But for the most part in New York sports, it's in the upper deck and the bleachers. Rarely are those areas filled with phonies who are there just to be seen. Cameras rarely make it to the upper tiers. Those individuals or celebrities looking for exposure are usually in the front

things
ISLANDERS FANS
hate

FISH STICKS LOGO
One of the worst logos ever created.
Thankfully, it didn't last long.

row on their BlackBerries or waving to the camera while on their cell phones behind home plate. Down in the premium seats, where tickets prices have surged beyond reach, the everyday New York sports fan has been priced out. It has all become corporate near the court, field, and ice. Subsequently, that's the place where you're a lot more likely to encounter someone who knows absolutely nothing about the game or either team. It's where you're likely to see patrons completely ignoring the game taking place literally five feet in front of them. If you're sitting there, you're probably more likely to hear about *American Idol* voting than All-Star ballots.

Some places, especially newer stadiums and arenas, often turn into hangouts rather than pure sporting venues. They become a place to party and enjoy a nice evening, not just a place to watch the home team win. Phony fans come to hang with their friends, drink, and enjoy the amenities. The game becomes a sidenote for some, who often don't care to see the game and have no stake in who wins. By all means necessary, avoid this type of crowd. Steer clear of sections that are filled with frauds and head to the places where the result of the game actually matters.

Most of the time, that's upstairs. That's where many of the hardworking, real New York sports fans hang. They're up there for a reason too. They want to be seated with their people.

Where the Real Fans Sit

Here are some areas in local stadiums or arenas where the game, not the scene, is the number one priority:

The blue seats at MSG. The seats aren't actually blue anymore but the Rangers fans in the 400 level are still rowdy and loyal to a fault. The denizens there are credited with inventing some of the most popular and famous chants, such as "Potvin Sucks." So simple, yet classic. Home of the working-class Rangers fans, the occupants care about one thing: winning. That's why it's where the real New York faithful want to be seated.

The right-field bleachers at Yankee Stadium. This is where the "Bleacher Creatures"—a group of die-hard fans who clamor desperately for their team to win—reside. On top of being insanely loyal, they're also innovative with their cheers and chants. They are in charge of the stadium "Roll Call" that takes place at the start of each game. During the top of the first inning, the crowd will run through the roster, chanting each starting Yankees player's name (excluding the pitcher and catcher) until he acknowledges the crowd with a wave.

things NETS FANS love

DR. J
Julius Erving is the best player in Nets history. Plus, that afro is as memorable as the high-flying act.

Behind the end zones in the upper deck at Jets games. There was a time when the crowds at the opposite ends of Giants Stadium used to compete against each other to see which side could do a louder, "J-E-T-S, Jets, Jets, Jets!" While that has become orchestrated and corporate too, the sections are still filled with some hardcore fans.

RULE #22

VISITING FANS SHOULD BE SEEN, NOT HEARD

Entering the lion's den is a dangerous proposition. In fact, it's asking for trouble. Be careful whose territory you invade without an invitation. Your life could be in very grave danger.

Visiting fans are welcome—just so long as they don't cheer aloud.

This is true at stadiums around the country, some more so than others (McAfee Coliseum in Oakland, Lincoln Financial Field in Philadelphia, and Ralph Wilson Stadium in Buffalo, for example). If you're going on a road trip, be careful. Be seen but not heard, for your own safety. Wear your jersey proudly, but try to keep the smack talk to a minimum.

There is just no need to incite the crowd. You're grossly outnumbered and you could end up being the fan dragged out by security. You also don't want to be the fan getting kicked in the head by a crowd of home-team supporters. Keeping low key at visiting stadiums decreases your chances of being involved in such an incident.

For many real New York sports fans, staying mum is not easy. By nature, most are loud and boisterous; they enjoy rooting for their team with authority. On the road, that's just asking for trouble. On the road, being there is enough.

For those coming to New York for a game, the same holds true for you. Do yourself a favor and be seen, not heard.

RULE #23

NEVER DO THE WAVE, MACARENA, OR CHICKEN DANCE

Come on, guys. This is amateur hour kind of stuff. It's reserved for the Jacksonvilles, Carolinas, and Tampa Bays of the sports world, not New York with its immense, knowledgeable base of real fans. Die-hard New York sports fans don't engage in such foolishness. It's embarrassing. Lame dances or faux cheers don't belong in stadiums in the Tri-State area. Luckily, for the most part, they don't occur. Let it remain that way.

RULE #24

KEEP THE NOISEMAKERS AT HOME

New York sports fans don't need help making noise. They are loud by nature. They are real, and so are their emotions. Expressing themselves has never been a problem—just ask the Boo Crew.

Don't even bother bringing the thunder sticks, air horns, clappers, cow bells, megaphones, or vuvuzelas. (For those of you unfamiliar: the vuvuzela is a plastic horn which is commonplace at soccer games in South Africa. Its constant buzzing sounds like a swarm of insects, and the sound rings in your ears for hours afterward. In short, it's brutal.) None of those accoutrements are necessary. Your voice and lungs can do all the damage necessary.

RULE #25

DON'T COME WITH WEAK SIGNS OR CHANTS

Real New York sports fans go hard or go home. They don't bring any weak stuff to the stadium or arenas. If you're going to bring a sign or start a chant, make sure it's clean and make sure it's good. It doesn't have to be too complex; some of the best and most popular chants in New York sports history have been quite simple. Consider the following:

"Joe Must Go." "Fire Isiah." "Potvin Sucks." "1940, 1940, 1940." "Darryl, Darryl." "Let's Go Mets." "De-Fense." "Who's Your Daddy?" "Good-bye Allie, good-bye Allie, good-bye Allie, we hate to see you go."

Nothing fancy there, just solid and true. And what makes them so special is that real New York sports fans mean what they say. Jets fans really wanted Joe Walton to go. Somewhere, anywhere

Keep Rule #25 in mind, because when you go to the stadium, you are what you write.

102

but New York. Knicks fans desperately wanted Isiah Thomas
fired. Rangers fan really thought Denis Potvin sucked (maybe not
as a player but as a person). Islanders fans were correct in that
the Rangers had not won the Stanley Cup since 1940. Giants
fans meant it when they were preparing Allie Sherman for his
good-bye.

Real New York sports fans are even willing to go the extra mile
if necessary. The Giants' dreadful teams of the '60s and '70s
had the fans regularly chanting "We've Had Enough." But that
wasn't enough for one fan, who hired a plane to fly above the
stadium holding a banner that read: "15 Years of Lousy Football,
We've Had Enough."

That's the way to send a message. That's bringing it hard.

RULE #26

NO SCOREBOARD MARRIAGE PROPOSALS

Admit it, this tactic is lame. You have more imagination than this.
Don't you? How many people before you have used the same
ploy?

In case you haven't realized this, the reaction from most of the
fans in the wake of these scoreboard proposals is roughly akin
to what occurred when the Giants' Lawrence Taylor popped the
bone out of Joe Theismann's leg on national television: everyone
is disgusted by what they're seeing but they feel the urge to look
anyway.

We do know some instances where these proposals come
onto the scoreboard before or after a game and not during the
course of the action. That is somewhat more reasonable. If you
have to do it, then at least have some decency and do it then,
will you?

PART SEVEN

BOOING AND CHEERING

RULE #27

BOO ONLY WHEN IT'S APPROPRIATE

The thin line between displeasure and disgust was tested when Derek Jeter started the 2004 season 0-for-10 at the plate. The same Yankees fans who cheered him so many times over the years were not happy as the slump crept to 0-for-11, 12, 13, 14, 15...and it didn't stop there.

At some point, as the team as a whole stumbled through the opening week, the fans' displeasure meter tilted toward the far end of disgust. The needle had reached its absolute maximum. That's when boos starting raining down on Jeter—the same player who had a career batting average well over .300, the guy who helped guide his team to four World Series titles in five years and always did everything possible to experience ultimate success, including run face first into the stands in order to catch a foul ball. Yes, the great Derek Jeter was getting booed, and deservedly so.

"I'd boo myself," Jeter said during the shocking hitless streak that would eventually reach 32 at-bats before it ended with a home run. It wasn't the first or last time Jeter would flail through a stretch of ineptness. It also wasn't the last time the Yankees

FAN TIP

Booing is fine. Just leave out the obscenities. There are always kids in the building.

faithful showered their captain with their famed "Bronx cheer." Jeter received the same reaction during a difficult series against the Red Sox in '08. Again, the Yankees captain shrugged off the incident as little more than an occupational hazard. "What were you expecting, cheers?" Jeter explained that time around. "I don't think it was anything out of the ordinary."

Nothing out of the ordinary in New York at least, where the demands and stakes are significantly higher than any other market in the country. Arguably more than all other fan bases, New York sports fans want their team to win. Badly. That's why they're so demanding, even from players who have proven themselves to be among the greatest of all time.

This is a market, after all, that once booed the legendary Mickey Mantle. They even booed Roger Maris midway through his record-breaking run for the single-season home run record in '61. It just goes to show that if legends such as Maris, Mantle, and Jeter can get booed, anyone is fair game to New York sports fans. That is, *if* they are not doing their job properly. In that case, everyone is open to derision.

Mets, Knicks, Nets, Rangers, Devils, Islanders, Giants, and Jets fans have done their fair share of booing too. They have booed great players, bums, dogs, slackers, gritty guys, overachievers, and steroid freaks. They have booed players, officials, coaches, mascots, management—anyone and everyone under the sun. Clearly, they do not discriminate.

There is nothing wrong with voicing your displeasure, as long as it's deserved. As Jeter noted, no matter how much goodwill a player has banked, nobody is going to cheer a strikeout. Cumulative poor performance correlates directly to boos. It's one of the things that New York sports fans bring to the table and what sets them apart from a lot of fans: they are loud, boisterous, easily excitable, and volatile. It's just a part of our internal makeup. There is no way around it. The key is determining when it is and when it is not appropriate to boo.

It's okay to boo a player when...

...he's performing poorly.

How poorly? An 0-for-32 slump certainly qualifies, but if a player like Jeter is hitting well and then one night goes 0-for-3, that is a completely different story. In the latter instance, vociferously expressing your displeasure is inappropriate. A hitless night on its own is nothing; there needs to be an established precedence of failure to boo a normally productive player. For instance, A-Rod's continual failures in clutch spots prior to 2009 left him open to the fans' harsh criticism when he came up empty in the late innings. Rodriguez had shown a consistent lack of production in that arena. But booing Carlos Beltran for an isolated ninth inning strikeout or Tiki Barber for a rare fumble would be beyond the pale.

...he's not giving maximum effort.
Roberto Alomar was the ultimate dog for the Mets. Watching him play was just brutal; he was arguably the worst free-agent acquisition in Mets history. It seemed like he would rather have been in the clubhouse napping than on the field playing. That kind of obvious disinterest doesn't play well in New York. The 12-time All-Star never hit above .266 in his 1½ seasons with the

things
YANKEES FANS
hate

JASON GIAMBI
He underperformed and embarrassed the franchise with his steroid admission.

things
DEVILS FANS
love

JOHN McMULLEN
Hey, he brought the Devils to New Jersey in the first place.

Mets and was also shaky in the field. Not surprisingly, his stay in New York was short, and filled with lots of boos.

...he acts inappropriately or greedily off the field.
Despite helping the team win Super Bowl XLII as its top receiver and catching the game-winning touchdown pass, if Plaxico Burress ever returned to the Giants, boos would be appropriate. Burress derailed the Giants' '08 season by accidentally shooting himself in the leg with an illegal handgun. This came shortly after he was suspended two games for failing to show up to practice and not contacting the team for several days. An attitude problem in your team's clubhouse, someone whose personality or off-the-field antics threaten the welfare of team, qualifies him as a prime target for boos.

The Boo Crew
There have been plenty of reviled characters to come through the ranks of our Tri-State area teams. But it's hard to imagine anyone more despised than Knicks general manager/coach Isiah Thomas. Thomas, along with some other undistinguished players and personnel, makes our hall of shame.

Isiah Thomas and Stephon Marbury. For a few years, the Knicks fans packed the stands strictly to boo this doomed duo. That, and to chant, "Fire Isiah." The treatment was well deserved. Both Thomas and Marbury were incompetent on *and* off the court during their time with the Knicks. Thomas was embroiled in a sexual harassment suit that cost the franchise more than $10 million in penalties. Marbury allegedly refused to play and fought with management until he was finally released from the team.

Dave Brown. The quarterback out of Duke was the top pick in the 1992 supplemental draft, but never won over the Giants fans. His play probably had something to do with it, as did being the one to follow Phil Simms and Jeff Hostetler. The Giants had the worst offense in the NFL with Brown under center in 1996. To add insult to injury, Brown, then leading the Arizona Cardinals, swept the Giants during the '99 season.

Joe Walton. This Jets coach actually had some pretty good teams. But toward the end of his tenure, he was hated with a blistering passion. Jets fans showered him with relentless "Joe Must Go" invectives. Getting caught on camera picking his nose didn't help either; it just added to the perception that he was a dope.

Ed Whitson. It got so bad for Whitson that the Yankees passed him over in several of his home starts! It wasn't just his poor performance that sparked the vitriol. He was also involved in a fight with manager Billy Martin that left his skipper with a broken arm. Not surprisingly, Whitson's Yankees career didn't last very long.

Kenny Rogers. He was booed by Mets and Yankees fans because he was bad with both teams. The problem was, he was pretty good everywhere else. Mets fans definitely harbor more animosity toward him, since he walked in the winning run to end a playoff series against the Braves in 1999. Rogers was booed out of New York because it was a place where he just couldn't pitch.

Tom Poti. The defenseman was never a favorite of Rangers fans during his three-year stint with the club. At one point, it got so bad that he was booed by the home fans every time he touched the puck and cheered each time he left the ice. As if it were possible, his popularity took even more of a hit when he left the Rangers for the Islanders in the summer of 2006. He didn't fare well there either. Soon enough, he was gone from there, too. Poti was later a member of the Washington Capitals team that rallied from a 3–1 deficit to beat the Rangers in seven games during the first round of the '09 Eastern Conference playoffs. When asked during the series about the fans' wrath: "I could care less about any of that," Poti said. It's fair to say that Rangers fans probably share the sentiment.

Alexei Yashin. The Russian center came to the Islanders with high expectations. He got paid like a superstar and performed like an ordinary player. He never topped 75 points on the Island after notching 88 and 94 in his final two seasons in Ottawa. His production, or lack thereof, earned him plenty of boos from the home crowd. The Islanders eventually had to buy out the nearly $20 million that was remaining on his contract.

RULE #28

NEVER OPENLY ROOT FOR YOUR TEAM TO LOSE

So now you know when to correctly voice your displeasure. Next is determining when it could be permissable to want your favorite team to lose (but most of the time not even really admit it). Sure, it sounds weird. It is strange to think you might want your team to lose, especially if it's against one of their top rivals. But there are times when it is necessary.

It sounds amoral to want your enemy to win, doesn't it? How could a die-hard Giants fan root for them to lose against the hated Cowboys or Eagles? How could a Knicks fan hope his team falls to the Celtics? It goes against everything you stand for. You're faithful, passionate, loyal, ethical, and honest. You're steadfast in your beliefs. You're a winner who wants to do whatever is necessary in order to achieve ultimate success. You never give up.

But Rosie Perez's character said it best in *White Men Can't Jump*: "Sometimes when you win, you actually lose. And sometimes when you lose, you actually win." Say what? Stay with us. There are times in sports when this is proven true. When the Jets won their '07 season finale 13–10 in overtime on a snowy afternoon at the Meadowlands over the Kansas City Chiefs, they really lost. The Jets were 3–12 going into the game, and obviously headed nowhere but toward the top of the NFL Draft. That win, however, left the Gang Green with the sixth pick in the 2008 NFL Draft instead of the third pick. Atlanta drafted Matt Ryan third; the Jets settled for Vernon Gholston. Giants fans, meanwhile, were happy their team lost the last game or two in the '03 season. It helped the Giants finish 4–12 and get the fourth pick, which they used to draft Philip Rivers, whom they eventually traded for Eli Manning. That's worked out pretty good for Big Blue so far. (And the Chargers, too.)

things
YANKEES FANS
hate

FAT TOADS

It's fair to say Hideki Irabu wasn't George Steinbrenner's favorite player or his best investment.

Rooting for your team to lose really only works in the NFL and MLB. In the NBA and NHL, losing increases your chances for a better pick, but there is still a draft lottery. Only in the NFL and MLB, where the draft is geared to provide help for the long-term future, is draft order determined strictly by record, thus making losing in the last week of the season for the betterment of the franchise in some cases. In those rare circumstances, and those instances alone, it is okay if you want your team to lose.

However, do not under any circumstances openly root for them to lose. Therein lies a big difference. Remember, giving outward cues of your fandom is key. It's why you wear the jersey. It's why you cheer. Maybe concealing that desire for a better draft position is being phony and fake, but we just can't imagine

Cheering Faux Pas

There was one time when I guess I broke Rule #28 and rooted against my team. I blame Bernard King. I loved him as a player—and the Knicks let him go after he got injured. He came back with the Bullets and he scored 49 against the Knicks in '91. That was the only time I rooted against the Knicks. I rooted for King that night. I was angry at the way it all ended with him in New York after he hurt his knee. He and Ewing should have played together. The way they let him go always upset me. So I was kind of glad that night with the way he stuck it to them.

Don't get me wrong, when the Bullets met the Knicks in the playoffs later that season, I was cheering for New York all the way. But I still had a soft spot for King. He got a raw deal with the Knicks. —JB

cheering for, say, the Jaguars when they're playing the Jets at Giants Stadium. Not even a golf clap for Jacksonville would seem appropriate. Just some sort of concession like, "Okay, it's better that they lost." Nothing, and we mean nothing, should make you cheer another team's success over your own. Got it?

RULE #29

NEVER ROOT FOR FANTASY SPORTS OVER REAL SPORTS

This brave new world we live in has changed professional sports as we know it. We now live in fantasyland. Everyone seems to be involved in one, two, or three fantasy leagues. Your office has one. Your buddies from college. Your friends from the gym. Your pals from childhood. It's almost impossible to keep it all straight, isn't it?

This fantasy sports landscape has created quite a dilemma for some sports fans. It's gotten to the point at which fantasy interests have blurred actual team interest. Sometimes it's even hard to distinguish the difference. Do you want to beat your friends, coworkers, and family more than you want your favorite team to win? Is winning usually rather small sums of money in a fantasy league more important than seeing your team win? You might say that it depends on how much money. But unless it's a life-changing sum, you should stick with the real world, not fantasy. After all, you've been with your favorite team much longer.

What's disturbing is that it's becoming more and more common for individuals to forgo their established rooting interests for their fantasy teams'. For a real New York sports fan, that notion is inexcusable. We would never do that. Allegiance to team first, fantasy second. A Giants fan, no matter the score, can't be rooting for Donovan McNabb to score a touchdown against the Big Blue defense because McNabb is his fantasy quarterback. It doesn't matter if the touchdown is meaningless to the final score or not—you just shouldn't do it.

In conjuction with the flip rule: you should also bear in mind that you should not change the channel during your team's game to watch a player on your fantasy team. You should be watching the entire game involving your favorite team from start to finish. Flipping channels is an egregious offense, but particularly so if you're checking in on your fantasy roster.

Unfortunately, fantasy sports is taking over professional sports. Some fans are taking it so far that they are actually willing to sever ties with their real-life team (most often, during tough times) in favor of their fantasy teams. Clearly these people can't be real New York sports fans. If anything, they're fans of "fantasy."

RULE #30

WHETHER YOU'RE CHEERING OR BOOING, BE LOUD

New York sports fans are vastly different from others around the country. In general, they're louder and more aggressive. And they should be. Any New Yorker will tell you that it's part of their nature. This should not change at games. Yell, scream, heckle, do whatever you please (as long as you keep it clean) when in a stadium or arena. That's part of the reason you're there in the first place, so you can express your disgust or pleasure like a complete lunatic without your spouse or partner dispensing nasty looks in your direction.

Don't worry about the person behind or in front of you complaining. It's all a part of being at a game. Fans pay money for tickets so they can voice their approval or displeasure at what is happening on the field, ice, court, or diamond. Real New York sports fans do it loudly.

RULE #31

DON'T CHEER FOR THE VISITORS

When you attend your team's game, you're there to support them, to cheer on the team and its players. You're not there to support the visiting players, no matter how great they are. Sure, you can show respect to them by acknowledging great plays and performances, but don't—under any circumstances—root for them. And don't cheer to encourage them to do something great or spectacular. There is a very big difference between acknowledging good play by your opponent and rooting for it to come at the expense of your team.

During the '08–'09 season, a plethora of Knicks fans violated this rule. They cheered for both Kobe Bryant and LeBron James when the Lakers and Cavaliers came through the Garden. That's right, they cheered.

Kobe scored a Madison Square Garden–record 61 points in a February win over the Knicks and he was greeted with a standing ovation from a very large portion of the crowd when he was pulled out of the game in the fourth quarter. It wasn't a respectful standing ovation either. It was the same kind of applause Willis Reed got when he headed to the bench following his courageous Game 7 cameo in 1970. Spike Lee, the famous face of the Knicks fans, was laughing, clapping, having a good time as his favorite team got spanked by his good buddy Kobe. It was an embarrassing night for the real New York sports fans, the real Knicks fans in particular. Oh, the pain.

LeBron had a similar experience at MSG a few games later. He scored 52 points and fell short of a triple-double because of a technicality. Knicks fans were cheering for him to score, shoot, and complete that triple double. There was no standing ovation this time, but there was evident support for LeBron. Instead of Spike Lee, this time it was Chris Rock, also a Knicks fan, who was laughing, clapping, and enjoying the show a little too much from his courtside seat.

The LeBron cheering can be somewhat excused since some Knicks fans were doing it as sort of a recruitment stunt. Many Knicks fans hoped to land LeBron in free agency the following year. Regardless, it was inappropriate. It's never advisable for a New York sports fan to cheer for the opposition. And even when you're there and want them to lose (see Rule #28), you never openly root for your team to lose.

We can also do without Spike Lee sitting courtside in Los Angeles rooting for Kobe and the Lakers. Come on, Spike—represent!

No More Cheers

Cheering Kobe and LeBron in '09 was bad, but it could have been worse. Here are some visitors that never, under any circumstance, should have been cheered in New York.

things
JETS FANS
hate

THE MUD BOWL, DON SHULA, AND A.J. DUHE

Couldn't someone in Miami have put the tarp on the field? Apparently not if Shula had anything to do with it. Duhe was the beneficiary of three interceptions in the 1982 AFC title game.

Michael Jordan. Not even a courtesy clap. Jordan hated the Knicks with a passion and the feeling was mutual with New York fans. They hated it when Jordan came to town, probably because he torched them so often. Early in Jordan's career, New York fans gave him a standing ovation when, in his seventh game as a pro, he dropped 33 points in a little over three quarters before heading to the bench in a blowout win. Later there was the Double-Nickel Game, in which he scored 55 points in one of his first games back from retirement; the triple-double in a crucial Game 5 in '93 (the Charles Smith debacle); and a 47-point effort in an '88 regular-season game where he pulverized Ewing and knocked the Knicks out of the playoffs. And that's just a small sample of the damage Jordan did at MSG.

Randall Cunningham. It must have been some sort of foreshadowing that Cunningham's first career game was against the Giants because he killed them over and over again. His eight career rushing touchdowns against the Big Blue were more than twice as many as he accumulated against any other team. There was the 91-yard punt in '89 at Giants Stadium, the amazing escape of Carl Banks and off-balance TD pass that followed in '88, and two victories off the bench in his last season with the Eagles in '95. Then, in his last career game against the Giants, when he was quarterbacking the Minnesota Vikings, Cunningham even beat them in a dramatic Wild Card

things
ISLANDERS FANS
love

THE LIGHTHOUSE PROJECT

The embattled development project that includes a new coliseum and would keep the Islanders on Long Island.

Game. It didn't matter what jersey Cunningham was wearing. He was a Giants killer.

Don Shula. Sure, he's a coach, but he was as great a foe (probably even more so than Dan Marino) for the Jets as any player who took the field against Gang Green. Shula is believed to have been responsible for the missing tarp before the Jets' 1982 AFC Championship Game in Miami. The Jets had a high-powered offense and their coach at the time, Walt Michaels, suggested Shula purposely misplaced the tarp to slow them down. The game was played on what *New York Times* columnist Dave Anderson wrote, "resembled a rice paddy." It was believed to be all Shula's fault. And that's just one game. He also led the Dolphins to plenty of other damaging victories against the Jets.

Roger Clemens. The fans at Citi Field wouldn't be too excited to see Clemens under any circumstance, unless he was going to get in a ring with two hands tied behind his back with Mike Piazza carrying a shredded bat in his hands. Clemens beaned Piazza in the head and then threw a bat at him during the '00 Subway Series. That transgression alone is enough to get him on this list.

Curt Schilling. That bloody sock, the constant ripping of New York, and his dominance during the '01 series with Arizona left Schilling persona non grata at Yankee Stadium. As if going 1–0 with a 1.69 ERA in three starts for the Diamondbacks in that memorable World Series wasn't enough, *then* he had to do the whole bloody sock thing?

Mario Lemieux and Sidney Crosby. Pick your poison. The Penguins stars killed everyone in their respective careers, but they saved some of their best (or worst) for the Garden. Lemieux once had a five-goal game at MSG. He also helped send the Rangers home in the playoffs all three times they met in the postseason. Crosby beat the Rangers in his first career playoff series and took major heat from the Rangers and their fans for flopping around the ice.

Scott Gomez. He's not welcome in New Jersey after he signed with the Rangers for more money in '07. Any other team but the Rangers would have been palatable; it was basically the Devils' decision not to sign Gomez to a lucrative long-term deal. But seeing him back there time and again...Gomez was booed every time he touched the puck.

Dale Hunter. Not a favorite at Nassau Coliseum—or anywhere else for that matter—because of his dirty play. Hunter crushed Pierre Turgeon well after Turgeon scored a goal in Game 6 of the '93 Patrick Division semifinals. The Islanders won that game and Hunter received the largest suspension ever at that time, 21 games, for the hit. Still, Turgeon missed most of the next round and was never the same when he returned that season, killing the Islanders' chances of returning to the Stanley Cup Finals.

PART EIGHT

AND DON'T FORGET

RULE #32

BE KNOWLEDGEABLE

When Carlos Beltran steps to the plate, real New York Mets fans know the deal. The team's Puerto Rican center fielder signed with the Mets as a free agent prior to the '05 season after putting together one of the best postseasons in major league history with the Houston Astros. Beltran signed a seven-year, $119 million deal and struggled in his first season with the Mets as he fought a quadriceps injury. It sapped his speed and power but he still went out there every day and worked hard. He then hit more than 30 homers and knocked in more than 110 runs for the Mets in '06 and '07 and was solid in '08 (27 homers and 112 runs) before missing a large part of the '09 season with a knee injury.

This information, available on the back of his baseball card, might seem highly detailed, but to the die-hard New York sports fan—and a Mets fan in particular—it's common knowledge. A true Mets fan can tell you all about Carlos Beltran—his history, injuries, and accomplishments. They are well versed on his abilities and his capabilities. They even know some basics about his life off the field. Several seasons of data collection makes this natural for a real fan. It doesn't take studying or research;

Beltran's stats are absorbed because of everything we see and hear over the course of several seasons.

The announcers tell us stories about Beltran's work ethic. The papers write about his loyalty to Puerto Rico during the World Baseball Classic. Beltran reveals volumes about himself during interviews, both in what he says and how he acts. This is the way we learn about our New York sports figures. The longer they stay, the better we get to know them. We learn a little more about Beltran, David Wright, Jose Reyes, Mariano Rivera, Derek Jeter, Eli Manning, Martin Brodeur, Henrik Lundqvist, and Rick DiPietro each year, and their backstories ultimately become common knowledge.

As it should be. Real New York sports fans put so much time and energy into their teams and players that they're bound to accrue plenty of knowledge about their team and its players along the way. It's why real New York sports fans know what they are talking about. They in turn know the team and its rosters like the back of their hand. It becomes like second nature.

What you should know:

The Basics. This includes the fundamental stuff: where the team plays; the name of the stadium or arena, the owner, general manager, manager; the team colors, logo, and jersey.

The History. This information is important because it puts everything else into perspective. For instance, Jets fans must know that the last time they won a championship was back in 1969 when they beat the Colts in Super Bowl III. Without that knowledge, you couldn't understand the Jets' mindset as they enter each and every season. It's also critical to know your team's legendary players, classic games, and past coaches. Those footsteps are the ones that today's players walk in.

The News. You must keep up to date with your team's latest signings, trades, roster moves, and transactions. Keeping abreast of injuries is also vital to understanding where your team stands.

The Players. Know at least most, if not all, of your team's roster. Football is difficult, since some players rarely take the field and there are at least 53 players on the roster, not including the practice squad. But you should at least know your starting 22. You should know the entire roster of your baseball, basketball, or hockey team. MLB's active rosters allow just 25 players, the NBA has 14 to 15, and the NHL up to 24. This is a manageable feat for any true fan.

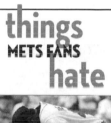

ARMANDO BENITEZ

The poster boy for frustrating 21st-century closers. Braden Looper and Billy Wagner are close behind.

The Rumors. Stay in tune with trade speculation. It's all over the radio, in the papers, and dissected around the water cooler. This stuff is vital information that provides insight into what your team's management is thinking and doing.

RULE #33

BE PASSIONATE

At root, it only takes one word to truly describe New York fans: passionate. Passion is the foundation of New Yorkers' fandom and what makes them so incredibly unique and special. Very few areas of the country can even come close to matching this unbridled affection, especially in the realm of professional sports.

things KNICKS FANS love

SPIKE LEE

A courtside fixture, his passion for the team is obvious.

What makes New York fans so passionate is the will to win. To most, a win isn't good enough; they want to crush the opposition. If the Yankees won six straight World Series titles, fans would still want a seventh. As if 27 entering the '10 season isn't enough already. How about giving someone else a chance? No thanks. Real Yankees fans don't care. They love their team, and they want to see them win every year. Period.

There are very few other fan bases that demand that kind of excellence from their team. But look to the other New York teams and you see the same expectation. Real New York sports fans, no matter their allegiance, support their teams with impressive enthusiasm. They want them to win by whatever means necessary. They demand success from the teams, players, and themselves. It's this dizzying passion and will to win that separates them from the pack. It's also the impetus that forces them to put in such a great emotional investment. Without this passion, the emotional investment wouldn't exist, and New York fans wouldn't be so special.

RULE #34

DON'T PUT MONEY ON YOUR FAVORITE TEAM

Some people consider betting on or against your favorite team a win-win situation. Far from it—most often it's lose-lose for the true fan. (Of course, we don't really condone gambling in the first place. Cough. Cough.) When you bet on your favorite team to win and they lose, it adds to the disappointment. And when you bet on your favorite team to cover the spread, and they do but they still lose the game, that's whipped cream on a poop sundae.

The only true winning scenario comes when you bet on your team to win and they do exactly that. Then all is right with the world, you're not depressed because of a loss, and your bank account doesn't take the hit. The problem is that this doesn't seem to happen too often, especially if you're a Jets, Mets, or Islanders fan. And then point spreads figure into the equation. Your team could win but not cover, or they could lose but still cover. So many options, so very few positive outcomes. There seem to be downsides to pretty much every situation except for one. It's no wonder there's that old cliché: the house always wins.

Betting on your favorite team is also bad karma. Most sports bettors (those who do it for fun, of course) have a much higher losing percentage than winning percentage. If they didn't, they'd be betting on games for a living. Since most bettors lose more than they win, they consider it bad luck to put money on their team. Some call this the Mush factor, after the character Eddie Mush in *A Bronx Tale*. Nobody had worse luck than Eddie Mush.

You never want to Mush your own team. In fact, if you traditionally have bad luck when picking games and you still have a desire to gamble, you're best off picking against another team.

RULE #35

...ESPECIALLY IF YOUR TEAM IS THE JETS

If history is any indication, this is a surefire way to go broke. The Jets are a frustrating franchise to its fans and the bettors. Gamblers who pick the Jets will likely lose several times each year in ridiculous, heartbreaking fashion. It's part of who the Jets are. Just imagine if you had money on the Jets in the Fake Spike Game against the Dolphins in 1994. What a disaster!

things
JETS FANS
love

BROADWAY JOE
He brought the franchise
respectability and had
the ultimate guarantee.

The Jets do what the Jets do. They continue to find unique and interesting ways to lose. They do things you've never seen done before by an NFL team every season. Usually, they are not good things—and that's not good for the bank account. Plus, if you're a Jets fan betting on your favorite team, it could prove detrimental to your health, adding stress from your wager to the strain you already feel watching your team struggle. Losing bets on the Cleveland playoff game thanks to Mark Gastineau's late hit, the Mud Bowl in '82, the Pittsburgh playoff loss in '05, the Fake Spike, Vinny Testaverde's late-game interceptions, halfback options, and countless other similar games could drive even a sane individual to a self-inflicted injury.

And even when the Jets win, they don't always win. Their Monday Night Miracle victory over the Dolphins in 2000 explains everything. The Jets had the second-largest fourth-quarter comeback in NFL history, overcame a 23-point deficit, won in overtime on a field goal and...pushed. For all that, even if you bet on the Jets that crazy Monday night, you wouldn't have won. They won by three points, matching the line. So if you did have money on that game, congratulations: you salvaged a push. All that nail-biting for a measly push. Guess it's better than nothing.

Don't think about taking the Jets in knockout pools either. As previously stated, when you want them to lose, that's when they win. Putting your money where the Jets are is a very dangerous proposition, no matter the wager.

RULE #36

DON'T SELL TICKETS TO RIVAL FANS

There's blue, orange, black, and red sprinkled throughout the Citi Field stands. Okay, the blue, orange, and black make perfect sense. Those are the colors of the Mets' uniforms. So why on earth are Mets fans seeing red? Oh, we get it. The red is from the Philadelphia Phillies fans who got their hands on tickets and made the trip north from Philadelphia. And they're all over the stadium. Their presence makes a difference. You can clearly hear cheers when something positive happens for the Phillies— when they score a run, turn a double play, get a key strikeout, or make a nice play in the field.

This is the scene that unfolds every time the Phillies visit New York. There is no way to stop it; it can not be stopped, it can only be contained. A similar scenario unfolds when the Mets travel south to Philadelphia for a visit, with Mets fans invading Citizens Bank Park. They make the 120-mile trip south just like Phillies fans do going north. Part of the reason for this visiting infiltration is some of the fans' greed and laziness. Local fans sell their tickets and, either directly or indirectly, they land in the hands of the enemy. That's simply the risk you take when you deal with ticket brokers. If a fan sells his seats to a ticket broker or on one of the websites that serves as the broker, anybody can buy them, including fans of the visiting team.

things
KNICKS FANS
hate

MICHAEL JORDAN

The reason the Knicks haven't won a championship since 1973. He absolutely killed the Knicks, along with everyone else in the NBA.

Real New York sports fans do not let that happen—especially in the postseason. They make sure, if they can't attend the game or are looking to make money, that the seats are purchased by a fan of their team. It's really not too much to ask. Just make sure those tickets end up in the right hands. After all, there is nothing worse than having a passel of visiting fans in your home stadium—especially if it's the postseason. In some cases, it can have a negative effect on the outcome of the game.

The Most Invasive Fan Bases
These teams get the most in-stadium support when they visit New York or New Jersey:

At Jets home games: Dolphins fans.
Where do they all come from? Was Dan Marino that charismatic that everybody just flocked to him and the Dolphins in the '80s and then never left? Were there that many frontrunners who hopped on the bandwagon when they went undefeated in 1972? It seems like there are more Miami fans in the Tri-State area than there are in South Florida. Getting a ticket for a Jets-Dolphins game at the Orange Bowl isn't that difficult, but keeping a Dolphins fan away from you at Giants Stadium is quite challenging. Where in the Northeast are they producing all these Dolphins fans? It there some cult that continuously spawns them? There must be because it just doesn't make sense otherwise. Fins fans aren't anywhere near as prevalent anywhere else in the country.

At Giants home games: Cowboys fans.
There is a reason they are nicknamed America's Team. Cowboys fans show up at just about every stadium around the country, and Giants Stadium is no exception. They show up in droves and are louder and more boisterous than any other visting team's fans. Making Eagles supporters look tame is not an easy feat.

Cowboys fans can do it. There are even some Cowboys bars and fan clubs in the Big Apple. Quite simply, the Cowboys have been a successful franchise for a very long time, and their fans have stuck with them through the decades.

At Yankees home games: Red Sox fans.
The Red Sox are similar to the Cowboys in that they have fans everywhere. And in the wake of their recent World Series title, Red Sox Nation seems to be multiplying. Boston fans definitely make their presence felt when the Sawks come to Yankee Stadium. After Boston overcame a 3–0 deficit and beat the Yankees with a 10–3 blowout win in Game 7 at Yankee Stadium in 2004, Red Sox nation was loud and proud in the stands. They celebrated vociferously and took over Yankee Stadium in the late innings of that game when the stadium started to empty out.

At Mets home games: Phillies fans.
The trip certainly is short enough. Just 120 miles separate the two cities, and Philly fans travel well. There is red throughout Citi Field whenever the Phillies come for a visit. The rivalry has become even more heated recently, ever since the clairvoyant Jimmy Rollins guaranteed the Phils would win the division in '07 and Philadelphia's Cole Hamels labeled the Mets "chokers." These guys are fierce rivals. Don't expect Philly fans to stop showing up any time soon.

At Knicks home games: Lakers fans.
There are a lot of Lakers jerseys, almost all of them Kobe Bryant jerseys of late, in the crowd when the team visits Madison Square Garden. Then again, there always have been. The MVP chants at the Garden for Kobe in '09 were loud, as was the standing ovation he received from the crowd. Of course Knicks fans gave them some help by playing terribly, but regardless, there were plenty of Lakers fans in the building.

At Nets home games: Lakers fans.
Their fans are everywhere when the team is good, and the
Lakers have been for a long time. Maybe there are just that many
George Mikan–turned–Elgin Baylor–turned–Jerry West–turned–
Wilt Chamberlain–turned–Kareem Abdul-Jabbar–turned Magic
Johnson–turned–Kobe Bryant fans out there in the world?

At Rangers home games: Canadiens fans.
Montreal fans somehow manage to fill entire sections at the
always sold-out Madison Square Garden whenever their team
comes for a visit. There are pockets of red all throughout the
arena for these games. Canadiens fans must travel really well
because there can't possibly be so many fans in the area. Can
there? If there are, then you don't notice it until the Canadiens
come to town. After all, it's not as if you see an overload of
Canadiens hats or jerseys around the city or in any borough on a
regular basis. Montreal fans must travel well. Second place goes

For the Love of the Game

Jim Lauterhahn is a little different than most sports fans. Different in a good way.

He views sports with a perspective that is foreign to many New York fans. To him, sports are there to enjoy and cherish. The die-hard Mets fan doesn't get stressed or angry when his team loses; he just watches with awe and admiration.

Sure, Jim wants his Mets to win, but that's just part of the reason he tunes in 120 to 140 times each season. He respects what the players do, whether they field or fumble a ground ball, hit a home run or fly out to the warning track. Jim keeps everything in perspective. He lets the manager manage and the GM do his job. The lack of pitching or a big left-handed bat? That's their worry, not his. Jim won't waste his time second-guessing the manager or calling for someone's head.

For Jim, it's about the game. The game that he loves and enjoys. He'd rather sit back quietly in his chair, listen to the game on the radio and soak it all in. What Jim is doing is simple: he's getting the most out of the game. It's a perspective that some over-the-top fans should consider. After all, Jim is doing what is most important: enjoying the game.

to Toronto and Pittsburgh fans, who also seem to find their way into New York and MSG in numbers.

At Devils home games: Flyers fans.
Most of the intruding fan bases are located in fairly close proximity, since it's practical for more fans to come when their foe is within driving distance. This is the shortest drive of all for the invaders—Philadelphia to North Jersey—and a big reason why Philadelphia fans swarm the Prudential Center. Plus, the Flyers have a rabid, dedicated fan base and tickets are usually easily accessible for Devils games, plenty of opportunity to capture a big section of the stands.

At Islanders home games: Flyers fans.
The drive and traffic out to Long Island don't stop the Philly fans from coming. They make their presence known at the Nassau Coliseum as well, even though the rivalry between the two teams hasn't been too vigorous since the early '80s. Still, much like New Jersey, getting tickets isn't all that difficult. In fact, it's been really easy to get tickets to Islanders games early in the 21st century.

RULE #37

ENJOY YOURSELF

This is why you do all the crazy things you do. It's fun, interesting, invigorating, and fulfilling. And you love it. Don't you?

Rooting for your favorite team is a national pastime. People have been doing it for hundreds of years. There is something that draws you to the games, stadiums, arenas, televisions, or radios. It's as if forces out of your control are pulling you in and there is nothing you can do to stop it from happening. You're defenseless against their powers.

What the powers are exactly is harder to identify. It could be the thrill of competition, the ups and downs, the excitement, the joy of winning, and the sense of accomplishment that comes with it. It could be the intricacies of the game itself, or its ability to distract you from the difficulties of everyday life. It's different for every one of us. Every New York sports fan has his own set of reasons for following his team.

The one common dominator, however, is that you enjoy it. Even though sometimes it might not feel that way, you take pleasure in rooting for your team. It's fun to listen to, watch, and attend games. Maybe everyone just wishes they could be on the field playing a game that they love. Or maybe they need to get the competitive juices flowing to feel alive. Or maybe it's affirming to have a shared purpose with a group of people. Whatever it is, it doesn't really matter. The important thing is that you honor the enjoyment, appreciate every minute, every *second* of your teams and the games. It's why you love sports in the first place. It's a fun hobby, passion.

PART NINE

CALLING ALL FANS

Considering the sources, it just wouldn't be right to do this book without laying down the basics that help make New York's sports talk radio, with 660 AM WFAN as its leader, the best in the country. After all, the FAN is the reason sports talk radio is what it is today. It was the world's first 24-hour all-sports radio station and its current popularity and influence in the nation's largest market are proof that several decades after its inception, not just a powerhouse but it is also an industry leader. It remains the trendsetter, always moving forward with the times, constantly improving and fine-tuning its product. While there have been a lot of imitators, none have matched or achieved the same success and clout of the FAN.

So, naturally, the standards for New York fans calling into WFAN are higher than anywhere else. More substance, style, and innovation are expected from each and every caller. Maybe in another town you can bring weak, inaccurate points or basic questions to the airwaves. Perhaps in Boston, Philadelphia, Dallas, Washington, and Miami they can't stop it from happening regularly. In New York we can, because that type of incompetence just doesn't fly with us—not on WFAN and especially not on the midday show with the FAN's fan as its host. As a matter of fact, it's not acceptable anywhere on the radio in the Tri-State area. Real New York sports fans are better than

FAN TIP

Be careful and don't go overboard. Otherwise you could be banned from the FAN's airwaves.

that. They typically follow the rules even when they don't know they are doing it. Call it innate ability.

That's why it's essential for them to bring their unrivaled knowledge, enthusiasm, and relentless desire to win directly to the FAN. It's not enough to bring these unique qualities to stadiums, parks, arenas, bars, and homes on a daily basis. Sports radio is an essential part of the fan experience. And that enthusiasm is required on the radio. It's demanded by the callers and listeners.

Most WFAN callers comply because they are knowledgeable, true New York sports fans. They may not even think about it, since they do it naturally. By following these unwritten rules fans have made FAN the nation's preeminent sports radio station. Subconsciously, they follow the guidelines that all New York sports fans should consider and keep fresh in their minds when calling the station.

No matter how antiestablishment you are, there is no way around it—there are rules to everything. Sports radio is no exception. Callers need to follow specific standards when trying to get on the air. No slacking, people. You just can't get on the air and say anything you want, anytime you want, to anyone you please. That's where the following rules come in.

RULE #38

BRING SOMETHING WORTHWHILE TO THE TABLE

The saying "different is good" is especially true in sports talk radio. Nobody wants to listen to the same point over and over again. *The Yankees need to move Joba Chamberlain back to the bullpen. They should keep him in the rotation. Wait, back to the bullpen. Stay in the rotation.* After the 10,000[th] time discussing the same topic, it becomes boring. We get it. Enough already. Move on to something else. Anything. That type of repetition can actually be used as a form of torture, not entertainment.

That's why it's especially important for quality New York sports fans to bring something different, unique, and worthwhile to the table when calling in to WFAN. As a station, they want listeners to say, "Hmmm, I never thought of that before," after they hear a caller, not, "No crap, who doesn't know that?" That is what makes quality sports radio: interesting callers. Bland and boring fans lead to unimaginative and flat shows and, in turn, fewer listeners. Fortunately, New York sports fans consistently bring good points, questions, and information to the airwaves, even during hours when most of the city is sleeping.

Part of what makes this possible is the real New York fans' exceptional knowledge. They know their teams, the intricacies of each sport, and much more history than the average fan. Whether it's because the New York teams have (for the most part) been around longer and have more history than most of their contemporaries is inconsequential. Not many fan bases around the country can come close to matching the amount of historic information consumed and retained by New York sports supporters. Every Yankees fan knows about Babe Ruth, Joe DiMaggio, Mickey Mantle, Yogi Berra, and the string of

things
KNICKS FANS
love

PATRICK EWING
He turned the franchise around and gave us some memorable series and seasons.

championships. The Yankees shove it down your throat (not that anyone really minds) in the new Yankee Stadium; it's just as much a museum as it is a ballpark, with its nostalgic touches everywhere. Monument Park is, literally, a museum of Yankees history. No matter where you turn, the new Yankee Stadium reminds fans of the team's history and helps educate its fans.

The Yankees' tradition of excellence raises the bar for other teams in the area, inspiring fans to hold themselves to an equally high standard. That's why, when phoning into WFAN, each caller comes with very high expectations. All fans who dial the station, no matter the topic or the time of day, are required to be knowledgeable on the subject they broach. If they want to get on-air, they should know what they're talking about. They have to bring something that at the very least is good, if not great, to the table. Fall short of these expectations and the call will be short.

1994

Erased the frustration of a 54-year championship drought.

To those of you who wonder what really makes a quality caller, consider the following tips.

Be Accurate. You can't just call the FAN and expect to be taken seriously, especially if your information is incorrect. This is the most basic prerequisite for talking sports in general. Be accurate and precise with your data. And if you don't know it, look it up. Either that, or put the phone down. Immediately.

If your point is that Derek Jeter never had a clutch hit in his career because he was 0-for-10 in the last week with runners in scoring position, you're going to get laughed off the air. Hell, you might send motorists straight into the Hudson River. The most recent numbers might support your statement, but historical empirical evidence strongly refutes the shortsighted claim. Jeter has had countless clutch hits in critical moments throughout his career. He hit a walkoff home run in Game 4 of the 2001 World Series, led off Game 4 of the 2000 World Series with a home run off Bobby Jones on the first pitch of the game, hit the Jeffrey Maier-aided homer in the '96 playoffs against the Orioles, and is called Captain

CHUCK BEDNARIK
The mean SOB knocked Frank Gifford out of the game—and out of football for almost a year.

Clutch for a reason. Those are just a few. Jeter has enough clutch hits in his career to fill a book by itself. So don't come to the FAN with a boneheaded statement like, "Derek Jeter never had a clutch hit in his career" unless you want to be classified alongside Mike Tyson, Jessica Simpson, and Stephon Marbury among the world's dumbest individuals. It instantly downgrades your credibility as a caller. Accuracy rules.

Be Knowledgeable. For a New York sports fan, the basics are always demanded. If you're going to call WFAN about the Mets, you better know they won the World Series in '69 and '86 and be able to tell anyone the basics about Tom Seaver, Dwight Gooden, Darryl Strawberry, Mike Piazza, and Johan Santana, regardless of your age. This is common knowledge for any real fan and quality caller. You better know that Piazza was the best catcher in the franchise's history and Seaver was a Hall of Fame pitcher. Lacking basic knowledge like this is disgraceful for someone who calls himself a true Mets fan, and particularly egregious if you're calling the FAN about the Mets. You can't possibly make a coherent point without this basic knowledge.

If the only thing you know about baseball is the Mets, how can you possibly call in about a trade scenario? You don't know anything about the Mets' possible trade partners. Your knowledge of pitcher Roy Halladay is at most what is on the back of his baseball card. Without the requisite knowledge of the entire landscape of a topic, calling the FAN is a waste of time. You simply won't be at the necessary level to hold an intelligent conversation with any host on any subject.

Take the Proper Tone. This often goes overlooked, but it just doesn't make good radio when the caller loses his cool or starts yelling at the host and doesn't allow for a two-way conversation. It's all right to get excited when making a point, but don't yell and berate the host. Most times, that's going to get you thrown off the air. Cool, calm, and collected is the way to go.

Bring the Necessary Stats. Sometimes you have to bring a little something extra to the table in order to make a point. In sports, statistics are often the empirical evidence needed to convince someone of your point of view.

Be Unique. The best callers don't just reiterate what's been said before them, they bring a fresh observation to the table. Granted, in a sports market that's saturated with media, it's not always easy. But as listeners of the FAN have proven time and again, there are plenty of people in New York who have that special ability to think outside the box regularly. They're innovative and not afraid to try new things. Fresh insights are found all the time.

Know the Rules. Two sets of rules govern professional sports.

things
KNICKS FANS
love

ALLAN HOUSTON
AT THE BUZZER

Front rim, backboard, through the net, he sent the eighth-seeded Knicks past the hated top-seeded Heat in the '99 playoffs.

One set is for the players, the rules that are enforced by umpires and referees. The other is the set of rules that regulates the owners and general managers outside the game. It's your job to know the basics of both.

You don't call the FAN and ask the Knicks to trade Eddy Curry and his bloated salary for a rookie who is making $1 million per year. There is a salary cap and other restrictions in the NBA that prohibit such trades. You should know this. If you don't, you're just wasting everyone's time. It's an unrealistic trade, and a blatant violation of the rules.

things
YANKEES FANS
hate

THE DODGERS

Not many teams can say they beat the Yankees in multiple World Series, three to be exact. (Who cares if they met in 11?)

You also don't call to complain about a pass interference call against the Giants' Aaron Ross when you have no idea what constitutes the penalty. Know that face-guarding is legal before phoning the station to complain that it was a violation. Be positive that they can't use instant replay on balls and strikes before grumbling about it on the air. Sure, it's hard to keep current with the ever-changing rules, but it's what a good New York sports fan does—especially before calling the FAN on the subject.

Get to the Point Quickly. At the very most, a caller on the FAN gets a few minutes, and usually just a few seconds to articulate their thoughts. Each segment only lasts approximately 15 minutes, and there is an everpresent queue of callers waiting in the wings. Make sure you make your point clearly and expediently. Don't sputter or babble before getting to it. The "first time, long time" line is also unnecessary to start a call. We've all heard it before. And any praise heaped on the hosts' shoulders is nice, but completely unnecessary with the FAN's fan. Straight and to the point with some flair and originality is the way to go. We'll take your call every time.

RULE #39

NO RIDICULOUS TRADE PROPOSALS

This type of tomfoolery infuriates everyone, from listeners to hosts. It's painful. The Mets are not going to trade for Albert Pujols in his prime, and they are definitely not going to get him for significantly less than he is worth. It doesn't matter the offer, nobody is getting Albert Pujols in the best years of his career. He's the Cards' man. Some trades just aren't going to happen, especially if there isn't equal value headed the other way in return. It is completely unrealistic and foolish to waste even one second discussing it. Under no circumstance was the Albert Pujols of '09 available for a variety of reasons. Any baseball fan worth his salt should know this.

So fight the temptation of making your next million-dollar trade suggestion to the listeners of the FAN. Pujols is not coming to the Mets. He is not going to the Yankees either. Kobe Bryant will not play for the Nets or the Knicks. No team is going to take Luis Castillo's bloated '09 salary and powerless bat. The Knicks' Eddy Curry, with several years left on a bad contract, is untradeable. A highly touted prospect like the Mets' Bobby Parnell is not enough

things ISLANDERS FANS love

THE EARLY '80s
Four championships plus five
Stanley Cup Finals appearances
equals one dynasty.

to acquire Roy Halladay or Tim Lincecum. Let's be honest. Keep the ridiculous proposals to yourself. Don't make all the listeners out there dumber for having to entertain these thoughts.

The seven- or eight-for-one deals can also be permanently shelved. The notion is just as moronic and unrealistic. When is the last time a trade of this magnitude happened? With the Saints and Ricky Williams? The Vikings and Herschel Walker? And how did those work out? No team is going to trade its roster, or a large chunk of it, for one player—especially given past history. It's just too risky. So don't dare pose it on New York sports radio.

Basically, there are a plethora of reasons why a trade proposal can be asinine. Here are some to keep in mind before you broach them:

An Invaluable Superstar
Kobe Bryant, Sidney Crosby, Peyton Manning, Albert Pujols, and players like them will never be traded. Why would their teams, barring extenuating financial problems, ever want to move them? These guys are the faces of their respective franchises. They bring fans to games, sell tons of jerseys, almost always perform impeccably in the game, and are worth their high salaries because of their marketability and the success that accompanies their play. Unless one of them declares himself on the market, thereby giving the team no choice but to move them, the thought of a trade is completely absurd. (And this didn't even work with Kobe, remember?) Players like this are too valuable to their team—on and off the field of play. No matter the value offered, franchises usually won't willingly move bona fide superstars unless they absolutely must. Most of the time the superstars on marquee franchises just can't be acquired at any price. They are not on the market no matter the offer.

Salary Considerations
As the market fluctuates year by year and injuries and age make certain contracts unmanageable, just about every team

in every sport has a few unmovable players with bloated salaries. Nobody wants an aging Luis Castillo for $6 million per season. An overweight Eddy Curry at more than $10 million each year has no value to another team unless his contract is set to expire. (Only in the NBA, where they have a hard salary cap, do teams actually *want* bad soon-to-be-expiring contracts. And you wonder why the league is losing fans by the second?) No other team would dare go near Jets defensive end Shaun Ellis' $5 million-plus annual base salary for 2009, given his mediocre production. Bad contracts are everywhere and they affect trades. More often than not, they make trades in leagues with and without salary caps impossible.

Uneven Value
"Get rid of A-Rod," Alex Rodriguez's detractors declare. "A minor leaguer would be sufficient," cries one of his critics. Come on. Get real. The Yankees would under no circumstance make such a move. They are not going to trade one of the best players of the generation in the prime of his career for anyone—least of all someone who may or may not even make it to the major leagues. Maybe the Twins (who did just that with Johan Santana) or another small-market team would be willing, but not the Yankees or any team in New York. One-sided trades just don't work, especially when the values are drastically different between sides.

Value can be determined by two different factors in professional sports: talent and money. With the Yankees' deep pockets and no salary cap in baseball, the notion of trading A-Rod for someone unproven is unrealistic. Only in sports with salary caps—NBA, NHL, and NFL—is it worthwhile to dump talented players with high salaries for junk, so long as that junk has an expiring or much more reasonable contract. Regardless, no matter the situation, even value, whether it's money or talent, needs to be exchanged in a trade.

It's Unnecessary.

Yes, sometime there are moves that even the Yankees will not make. After signing first baseman Mark Teixeira to an eight-year, $180 million contract in the winter of '08, they did not trade for the best first baseman in baseball during the '09 season. The Devils, meanwhile, are not going to look for an All-Star goaltender until Martin Brodeur is either ineffective or retired. As long as Brodeur is around, he's going to command a hefty salary and deserves to start. Getting a goalie would be completely unnecessary and financially irresponsible, especially under a salary cap. Investing in two expensive goaltenders is absurd if you expect to build a complete, well-rounded team. It would be a blatant misappropriation of funds. Economics are part of the equation for every team, no matter the sport or its value and revenue. Even the Yankees franchise, whose swelling payroll is legendary, has financial boundaries, proving there are unnecessary acquisitions even for a team in their position.

Past History

Fool me once, shame on you. Fool me twice, shame on me. That adage holds especially true with trades. You just can't afford to move an aging All-Star center for a bunch of overpaid role players, like the Knicks did with Patrick Ewing, even if the veteran in question demands to be traded. This is the kind of move that can set a franchise back for years. It can put a team in salary cap hell. The next time the Knicks actually do have an aging All-Star player on their roster, you would hope they will have

things
METS FANS
hate

CHIPPER JONES

Larry enjoyed hitting against the Mets so much that he named his kid Shea. That's a slap in the face.

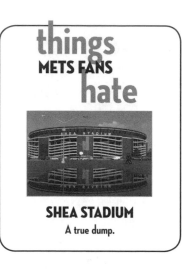

things
METS FANS
hate

SHEA STADIUM

A true dump.

learned from their past mistakes. They will suck it up for a year or two and just wait until that massive contract expires. Or so we hope, thanks to past history.

The rules of the NBA and NHL encourage such patience. The NFL is a slightly different beast. At a certain point, a team can release any player. That aspect, along with the frequency of injuries and lack of depth on teams' rosters are mitigating factors in why trading is so rare. The Jets' recent acquisition of Braylon Edwards is the exception, not the rule. Don't expect many, if any, trades while the season is taking place. History indicates that it's just not likely.

RULE #40

BE REALISTIC

You don't want to be like former WFAN regular Jerome from Manhattan, who would declare the Yankees "Done! Done!" even though they were comfortably in first place and on their way to a World Series title. Sure it's humorous and laughable to be that far removed from reality, but 99 percent of the time it's just plain foolish and unrealistic. It might be funny but you don't want to be that guy. Despite the fact that the Yankees dropped three straight games, their season is far from over. In fact, during much of Jerome's FAN-calling heyday, the Yankees did an awful lot of winning. Just imagine if they were anywhere near as bad as Jerome said they were.

And there are millions of Jeromes out there, though thankfully few of them are as vociferous. But Jerome is joined by countless other callers who commit the same indiscretion of exaggeration. They weigh the scale down to the floor with negativity and make totally unrealistic comments. Countless callers over the years buried Patrick Ewing beyond belief. They claimed Ewing was horrible, terrible, a complete waste of size and talent who always failed in the clutch. Believe it or not, Ewing was a perennial All-Star. He was named one of the 50 greatest players of all time by the NBA. Regardless of how many callers declared him one of the worst players in basketball, he was nowhere near such—especially when stiffs such as Chris Dudley and Brian Quinnett played on the same court. In reality, Ewing was one of the best players in the NBA for quite some time. Sure fans were upset that he and the Knicks failed in some really big spots, but it was Ewing's greatness itself that increased the standard by which he was judged.

Consider the fans on the opposite end of the unrealistic spectrum. These are the fans who are blinded by the propaganda, always believing this year, this game, this week, this day is going to be the time that their team miraculously erases all those years of failure and shines. They think it's only a matter of time before everything finally clicks with that underachieving player. Sometimes, though, you need to get over the dream scenario and enter reality. Sometimes it's just not possible. Unfortunately, miracles don't happen every day. When an inferior product is put out on the field, rink, or court, more often than not it's going to result in a loss. When a player puts forth sub-par performance after sub-par

things JETS FANS love

THE SACK EXCHANGE
Mark Gastineau, Abdul Salaam, Marty Lyons, and Joe Klecko led a defense that dominated. The Jets D hasn't been the same since.

things
YANKEES FANS
love

DEREK JETER

Model citizen, a great shortstop,
and an incredible leader.

performance, it's not likely that he'll become an All-Star overnight. Don't tell yourself otherwise, and don't expect you can do better yourself either. You can't hit a curveball, beat an NBA player off the dribble, skate circles around an NHL player, or absorb a big hit from an NFL linebacker. Sorry, but there are reasons you're not a professional athlete. Real New York sports fans know this all too well. They're not dreamers, they're realists.

RULE #41

NEVER QUESTION MY FANDOM

Want to see me lose my cool and defend myself like it's my family being attacked? Just have the intestinal fortitude to question my fandom. I dare you. Remember, I'm the same guy who used to spend almost all his time watching and rooting for his teams and calling into WFAN. You don't get paid to do any of that; I did it because I'm a die-hard fan.

Whether you disagree with my opinions is one thing, but to question whether I'm a fan is completely asinine. I root for my teams through thick and thin, through good times and bad (mostly bad considering I'm a Jets, Mets, Knicks, and Rangers fan), despite horrific ownership, pathetic leadership, financial hardship, and overall incompetence. I've experienced enough agita throughout my years of being a fan to last anyone a lifetime. Never, under any circumstance, would I stop rooting for my teams.

I have been there for just about every Mets loss and disappointment in team history. That's what happens when you've been around since the franchise's inception. I've cheered and rooted through a 120-loss season, two World Series titles, countless managers and GMs, and even multiple ownership groups. I've been there for every Jets game since Joe Namath arrived in the mid-'60s, basically since they dropped the moniker "Titans" and claimed the name "Jets." There have been plenty of bad losses since then. More than any Giants fan can possibly imagine, I'm sure. I've been there with the Knicks and Rangers ever since the mid-'60s, through season after season of close calls and disappointing playoff losses. Those damn Chicago Bulls. Oh, the pain. Through it all, I have never entered a year or season not ready, willing, and able to celebrate a championship. That unequivocally covers the necessary criteria of a fan.

Just because I'm a realist and I criticize moves, plays, and decisions by players and management in no way, shape, or form denigrates my fandom. In fact, it's exactly the opposite. I'm a fan because I care enough to criticize or defend every move, play, or decision. That's what real fans do. They form opinions—some positive, others negative. There just happens to be a lot of negative associated with my teams. To disagree with a move the team made in no way diminishes my support or enthusiasm.

Who said it is not a prerequisite to be an eternal optimist in order to be a fan? While there is nothing wrong with always seeing sunshine on a cloudy day, not everyone has to see the glass as half full. Most fans actually take the opposite approach, me included. I'm more glass half empty. Of course, if you're a listener, you probably know that already.

things
JETS FANS
hate

THIS SEASON
The next season
always looks better.

You Don't Know Joe

A lot can be said about Joe Benigno. He's too cynical. He's too pessimistic. He's too demanding. He's hard on his teams. This all may be true, but it's not necessarily bad. Joe is just a half-empty kind of guy. He might get criticized for it, but nobody will dare question his passion or his knowledge. All you need to do is watch him on a football Sunday and you'll be sold. Or just sit down with him at any time and talk sports. Joe's knowledge floats to the surface immediately. His passion is not far behind.

He can rattle off the details from a game that took place 20 years ago as if it was played just yesterday. He knows every player, coach, and owner who has ever had a role with any of his teams. Joe is the Schwab of New York sports, with sports knowledge that can only be matched by the similarly sick degenerate sports fans. It's all part of what makes him the prototypical New York sports fan. While I might not always agree with his ideas or opinions, I'll always respect his knowledge and dedication. I'll never question his fandom. —JR

But it certainly doesn't mean I'm not a fan. A real sports enthusiast understands that as long as you're always there for your team through the good times and bad, you're the real deal. I'm definitely always there. Don't question me on this one.

RULE #42

DON'T PREFACE YOUR CALL BY CLAIMING ALLEGIANCE TO MORE THAN ONE TEAM

Clearly, this is a blatant violation of Rule #1: Only One Team Per Sport. Yet because there are multiple local teams for each major sport, this faux pas still occurs. It happens over and over too. Way too often. This declaration usually infuriates the hosts, callers, and anyone else who takes pride in calling himself a true New York sports fan. How could it not? They're wasting our time and insulting our intelligence.

So just don't do it. Never. Say you're both a Mets and Yankees fan to the wrong host (you know, like one of WFAN's midday hosts) and the call could end rather abruptly. It's possible a die-hard Mets, Jets, Knicks, and Rangers fan might just hit the dump button before you even get your point across. Next thing you hear could be a dial tone ringing in your ear.

Depending on the host's mood, the preface might be all that is heard. After all, it says everything the listeners and hosts need to know: you are not much of New York sports fan at all. What interesting point or scintillating idea could follow such an asinine opening premise?

Don't leave yourself open to ridicule. It can all be avoided rather easily: just don't bring the I'm-a-fan-of-two-teams act when calling New York sports radio's No. 1 station. It's verboten there, just as it is with all true New York sports fans.

things DEVILS FANS love

LOU LAMORIELLO

Pairing the best general manager in the sport with the best goaltender is a lethal combination. Lamoriello's track record is close to flawless.

RULE #43

DON'T SERIOUSLY DENOUNCE YOUR TEAM

Similar to declaring two favorite teams, this is an instant credibility zapper. Nobody is going to believe that a true, die-hard New York sports fan is going to divorce his team on the spot for any reason. It would be a violation of Rule #4, for starters. A real fan would never dump the Mets because they were headed in the wrong direction. They wouldn't drop the Rangers because they despise Sean Avery's tactics and act. Don't even bluff. No one will buy it. And if they do, they'll just consider you a frontrunner, not a real fan.

DEVILS FANS

SCOTT STEVENS AND KENNY DANEYKO

These two defensemen ended the careers of anyone skating with their heads down. Good guys to have on your side of the bench.

While denouncing your team publicly is not anywhere near as egregious as declaring two favorite teams (partly because it's often just a threat), it's something that should be avoided when calling into WFAN. The airwaves are not the place where crisis specialists await to deter bridge jumpers. The people on the other end of the phone are merely sports talk show hosts. Appeasing angered fans and mollifying their fake threats are not in the job description. They are there to talk sports. There are always more pressing, current issues real New York sports fans need to discuss than the mental instability of some depressed and frustrated so-called supporter. So take the bluffs somewhere else and leave them off the airwaves.

RULE #44

SAVE THE SELF-PROMOTION

Believe it or not, it's not all about you. That's right, nobody wants to hear about your personal life and experiences. They don't care about your business ventures, who you know, or your personal website, Twitter account, or Facebook page. That's all way too much information. The listeners, not the host, are your audience and they don't care about your private life. Trust us. They are worried and interested about one thing and one thing only when they listen to sports radio. They want to hear about sports.

So many people, however, just can't help but talk about themselves. It's all me, me, me. I, I, I. They like to hear the sound of their own voices and many want to be the next FAN's fan. They view their two minutes on the air as an audition, and they try to get in as much as possible about their personal life as they do in their actual point. These callers are often in it for the self-promotion.

Sometimes a person's anecdotes are semi-interesting. But more often than not, people like to call with the "Do you remember I was the one who waved to you on the street in Manhattan three years ago?" comments. Come on, guys. Let's be real. You're almost always not anywhere near that important or memorable. Hopefully deep down you know this already.

RULE #45

DON'T CALL AS A GAG

If you're willing to spend 20 to 30 minutes waiting on hold to make an immature joke on the air, we can only tell you one thing: get a life. You have way too much time on your hands. Find a new hobby, take a walk outside, and stray from that room with padded walls. And don't forget to tell your mom you're going out and will be back in time for dinner.

Even if you do get through the station's screener and dupe the host, you still probably won't make it to the air. Here's a notice to you idiots: radio is on delay. That means if you're going to curse or say something inappropriate to get a laugh, the chances of it being heard is slim. You're going to get

**things
METS FANS
hate**

ROGER CLEMENS
One of the biggest asses to ever play the game. He threw at Piazza's head—then he threw a shredded bat at him too.

bleeped out and dumped off the air. Good work, buddy. You just wasted 20 or 30 minutes of your life acting like a buffoon. For what, again?

RULE #46

DON'T CHANGE NAMES

Before we're off the topic of idiots, this foolish move needs to be discussed. Some WFAN callers feel the need to use aliases. But here's the tipoff: anyone who uses a fake name couldn't possibly be a real New York sports fan. Real New York sports fans don't need fake names. They're man enough to get on the air and say whatever it is they have on their mind in a coherent, respectful way. They don't get banned in the first place. Of course, some of the fake names come from people who have been banished from the show already. Take the hint, fellas. You're not wanted, no matter what name you provide. Nice try, though.

RULE #47

COMMENT ONLY ABOUT THE SHOW ON WHICH YOU ARE CALLING

You can only be accountable for your own actions and words. It holds true in life and on sports radio. Don't call the WFAN midday show and complain about something that was said the previous afternoon during *Mike'd Up*. I can't be held responsible for something another host or caller said. It's not my responsibility to defend or criticize it. The best way to contribute to a show is to listen to the conversation that's happening. Period. If you have a bone to pick with another host's show, be sure to call them the next day. I'm not interested.

RULE #48

DON'T BLAME LOSSES ON THE OFFICIALS

In other cities around the country, fans continually cry about conspiracy theories in which the officials being the lone factor in a loss. Real New York sports fans should take defeat like men. They don't come on the FAN and cry about it, blaming the loss exclusively on the officials. They might complain about a call (and then usually for good reason) but they would never put the loss on a referee's shoulders.

Granted, the officials in the NFL and NBA in particular are horrific. They miss calls every game and pretty much every play. MLB umpires are not that far behind. Regardless of the sport, the in-game administrators of the rules possess too much control over each individual contest. They do have the power to control the outcome. In the NFL, they could call a penalty on every single play if they really wanted to. That's a lot of power in the hands of a few individuals. They get a lot right, but too many wrong.

Still, if a call doesn't go your way, it's not the end of the world. It's not the reason your team lost. There are hundreds of other plays and opportunities during the course of a game. One, two, or three bad or missed calls shouldn't be the only thing you're calling in to comment on. Save the whining for your own living room.

things
NETS FANS
hate

THE WESTERN CONFERENCE'S BIG MEN

Namely, Shaquille O'Neal and Tim Duncan. They have played a huge part in the Nets' failure to win an NBA Final, especially with Jason Collins guarding them.

things
NETS FANS
love

JASON KIDD
The triple-double machine brought excitement to the Meadowlands for the first time in years and led the Nets to a pair of Finals appearances.

The Knicks did not lose to the Bulls in Game 5 of their 1993 playoff series because the referees missed a foul call (or even two or three) as Charles Smith attempted several layups in the paint. It doesn't matter that if the situation was reversed, Michael Jordan or Scottie Pippen would have been standing at the foul line instead of absorbing serious contact in the paint. The Knicks lost because they did not make enough plays and free throws throughout the 48 minutes of action. They had 73 field goal attempts and 35 foul shots. How can you possibly blame the loss exclusively on the referees' decision to swallow the whistle on one play? The answer is you can't, and you shouldn't. Losses do not occur solely because of the officials.

So don't whine and deflect the blame elsewhere when calling the FAN after games like that. It's understandable to express your anger and displeasure, but you can't pin the whole loss on the referees. In the long run, the missed and blown calls will work out evenly. They will work in your team's favor just as much as they work against them, even though it might not seem like it.

The only exception to this rule would be if a referee, umpire, or linesman truly decides the game. Players should always decide the outcome. After all, that's why they get paid the big bucks.

Hall of Fame: Joe's Top 10 Favorite Callers
Some callers bring more to the table than others. These 10 FAN enthusiasts not only rarely break the aforementioned rules but they also often offer something special:

Doris from Rego Park. She's deceased, but she will live on in our memories forever. For years, Doris from Rego Park, with her trademark cough and limitless Mets knowledge, was a regular caller to the overnight show. Every time you heard her distinctive voice, it left a smile on your face. She brought unique, lucid ideas to the airwaves, and everyone respected her knowledge and loyalty to the Mets. You knew after that cough there was something insightful destined to follow. Doris was a favorite of everyone—hosts, producers, board operators, and fellow listeners and callers. How can you not love a caller who set her alarm for 1:00 AM every morning just to make her point on the overnight show? That's dedication.

Bruce from Bayside. He's not a fan of any of the New York teams. So what? It doesn't stop him from being one of the regulars who always brings something interesting to the air. Bruce is still probably the most knowledgeable caller on the FAN. Dubbed "the King of Useless Information," he knows as much sports as anyone. Just ask him. Or try to answer some of his toughest trivia questions. Maybe the reason he has so much useless information has something to do with the fact that his beloved Browns and Indians are rarely in the postseason.

Bruce from Flushing. A huge Yankees and Rangers fan, the two teams are Bruce's favorite topics, though he also talks Giants. He is as well-rounded as any caller on the FAN. He's always on-point and provides quality analysis and second-guessing. What else can a sports radio host ask for on a consistent basis?

things
KNICKS FANS
hate

TRENDY GARDEN

When the Knicks are good, the phony fans come out in droves for the courtside party. The same faces can be seen later in the week at Lakers games.

Short Al from Brooklyn. A true icon. An absolutely stellar caller, right up there at the top of the all-time list with Doris from Rego Park. Short Al was on the station so much over the years, especially while the working stiffs sleep, that he was almost as recognizable as the long-time hosts and update anchors. It didn't matter the topic or the time of year, Short Al always got in something about his beloved Brooklyn Dodgers. Oftentimes, that includes a tidbit about his favorite player, the legendary Jackie Robinson. While the Dodgers and Jackie are among his clear favorites, George Steinbrenner is very obviously not. Short Al liked to get in his licks about the Boss, and he did it often.

Lenny in Manhattan. There is no funnier caller than Lenny. He brings some much-needed comic relief to a traditionally charged sports-dominated environment. It's not surprising that Lenny's voice has been heard on *The Howard Stern Show* over the years. Still, despite his other interests on the radio dial, Lenny knows his sports. By no means is he just a one-liner machine. He also brings substance with his pizzazz.

things
YANKEES FANS
love

THE BOSS

George Steinbrenner wanted to win and did whatever was necessary to be successful. What else can you ask for?

Miriam in Forest Hills. There is no more devoted Islanders fan than this Queens resident. It doesn't matter that Miriam can't see the action. She can hear and absorb it all. When Miriam calls the FAN, she always has keen observations to share. She knows everything about the Islanders, undoubtedly more than any host. It probably has something to do with the fact that she almost never misses a game.

Brian in Rockville Center. Even though he missed the Thursday night Jets-Patriots affair during the

'08 season for an AC/DC concert, Brian is a quality Jets and Mets fan who is a regular on the FAN. Hey, everyone makes mistakes. Luckily, he brings a lot to the table every time he phones the station. Let's just hope a Celine Dion or Michael Bolton concert isn't the next scheduling conflict that forces him to miss a key game. That'd be difficult for us to let him live down.

John in Philly. You must be an incredible caller if you're a die-hard Philadelphia fan and still make this exclusive collection of names. You have to be a personable, affable,

things
RANGERS FANS
hate

MARIO LEMIEUX

Let's just say Adam Graves' slash to Lemieux's wrist in the '92 playoffs didn't upset many Rangers fans.

knowledgeable all-around great guy to make it happen. This is exactly the case with John in Philly. He's a quality sports fan who would rather get his daily fix from New York's WFAN than Philadelphia's WIP. There is a common bond that makes John's integration possible in the enemy's own backyard. His Eagles and our Jets both bring annual heartbreak. Maybe that's why we have such a soft spot for his calls.

Ira in Staten Island. His dedication to the Jets is well established. Who else travels to every game, including preseason? Heck, preseason football is a lot like nonalcoholic beer. It may look and feel the same going down, but ultimately it has no discernable effect. Yet attendance enhances Ira's extensive knowledge about his favorite team, which he brings to the air during his regular calls. He also brings an eternal optimism that often proves refreshing/disturbing during the Jets' traditionally turbulent season. He also gets brownie points for giving personal pregame tidbits over the phone like the weather conditions in opposing stadiums, uniform colors the Jets will wear that day, the inactive lists, and even an update on which kicker performs better in warm-ups. Who else provides that kind of in-the-trenches information?

Joey in Yonkers. Want the gambler's angle? Joey in Yonkers will give it to you when he's on the FAN. He always provides a slightly different take than your average sports fan because he's looking at everything from a monetary value perspective. Joey knows his stuff and is always attempting to make a profit from this knowledge. It doesn't matter if it's NFL or WNBA, he's willing to bet on it. If only this philosophy could somehow help Joey land a girlfriend. Lord knows, we've tried to help.

CONCLUSION

Being a complete, flawless New York sports fan isn't easy. So many rules, only so much time. For the most part, it takes years of learning and fine-tuning to reach the point where you're suitable for public viewing. Perfection sometimes takes a lifetime to achieve.

New York fandom is a culmination of a lifetime of living and experiencing being a passionate, loyal, and true fan. But before you graduate to advanced NY fanaticism, first comes the basics. Hold steady, the rest will eventually follow. The foundation of a good fan is established during an individual's adolescent stages, but the growth process continues well into the senior citizen days. Basically, it's a long, arduous road. So in case you're flustered or overwhelmed by the minutia, here is the ADD version:

New York Sports Fans' Cheat Sheet
1. Only One Team Per Sport
   I pledge allegiance to one team per sport. No ifs, ands or buts. Get this right and you'll be well-respected by the masses.
2. Select a Team by Age 13
   Pick a New York team and stick with it. Just be sure it's done before maturing into an independent adult, because once the choice is written in the book, there is no turning back.

3. Never Ditch Your Team

    You are who you are, forever. Whoever said people can change, they obviously weren't talking about real New York sports fans.

4. Associate With, Marry, or Raise the Enemy—Only If You Must

    Regardless of what some may insist, NY sports is not the be-all, end-all in life. There is nothing wrong with sleeping, living or associating with others who are "different."

5. Get Some Gear

    That T-shirt, hat or whatever is an easy way to flaunt your allegiance. Make sure you have something, anything.

6. Watch It

    Set the TV or radio so you can watch or listen to the games of your favorite New York sports team on a regular basis.

7. Get to the Game

    There is nothing like being in a Tri-State area stadium or arena. It's an experience completely different from sitting on a couch or barstool, and an itch that needs to be scratched at least once a year.

8. Know Your Role

    Cheer and boo at the appropriate times. In simplistic terms, for the most part, that means cheer your New York team and boo the opposition.

9. Be a Good Fan

    Remember the big picture. Being a New York fan is supposed to be a fun, enjoyable experience. Invest the requisite time and energy, but don't go overboard and let it guide your life.

10. Radio Rules

    New York sports radio is like no other. It demands a lot from both its callers and hosts. Make sure you're well informed and get straight to the point.

Now, to every rule-abiding New York fan out there, go forth and enjoy your teams!

APPENDIX

The Famous Fans

The Tri-State area teams are represented well on the wide-screen and the boob tube. Each New York area franchise has significant celebrity fan support. We're not talking about someone going to one game, throwing on a jersey for the camera, and proclaiming himself a fan. That's against everything that a die-hard represents. We're talking about real New York sports fans, ones who follow the rules set out in this book.

Each team has its own celebrity face. Some are better-known and more popular than others, but that doesn't mean they are the biggest or best fans. For the Knicks, it's Spike Lee and Woody Allen. For the Nets, it's Jay-Z. The Rangers had Christopher Reeve before his passing. The Islanders have *Entourage* star Kevin Connolly. The Devils can claim Newark native Shaq. Billy Crystal and Rudy Giuliani are most closely associated with the Yankees. Jerry Seinfeld is Mr. Met (no, not *that* Mr. Met). Jon Bon Jovi is the most prominent Giants fan. The Jets are represented by comedian Kevin James. Good company to be in. And among these famous fans, there are many more who show their support.

The Yankees

Sarah Jessica Parker. You've got to give the *Sex and the City* star some props. Her husband, Matthew Broderick, is a die-hard Mets fan. Parker stuck with the Yankees, remaining a fairly regular patron at the old and new stadiums.

Billy Crystal. One of the most famous faces seen fairly regularly at Yankee Stadium, the comedian and lifelong fan even made a movie about the Mantle/Maris home-run race. He has been highly involved in working with the organization, and was signed to a contract and awarded a charity at-bat with the team during spring training in 2008. The fact that he struck out doesn't diminish his fandom. The fact that he wore a Mets hat in *City Slickers*, however, does. Added to which, the team he co-owns, the Arizona Diamondbacks, beat the Yankees in the '01 World Series. Worry not, he has a viable explanation for both. The Mets helped him with a charity event during the making of *City Slickers*. And who wouldn't want to own a Major League Baseball team?

Rudy Giuliani. Typically, New York's elected officials do what is most politically correct. They rarely pick sides when it comes to choosing between the city's sports teams. But there's nothing typical about Giuliani. During his term as mayor he had a sign on his desk that read, "Yankees Fan-In-Chief." Raised a fan of the team in Brooklyn living just blocks from the Dodgers' Ebbets Field, he's since become a true-blue fan of the Yanks.

Chazz Palminteri. He grew up in the Bronx and starred in *The Bronx Tale*, so it's only natural that he's a die-hard Yankees fan. "Chazz from Bedford" even calls into the FAN every so often for a little Bronx Bombers talk. When asked about the possibility of throwing out the first pitch of a Yankees-Mets game at the Mets' new Citi Field, Palminteri agreed, only on the condition that the ball was a Mets-Yankees baseball. "I'll do it, but people need to know I'm a Yankees fan," he said.

Regis Philbin. Given the amount he talks about Notre Dame football, the Yankees may not be his No. 1 team. Still, it's obvious

The Fanatical Fan
Nicky Turturro, Actor

As he sat there eating lunch in his Yankees jersey and hat after guest-hosting on the WFAN midday show, Nick Turturro rattled off memory after memory of George Brett killing the Yankees in the late '70s and into the early '80s. There was no doubt the **NYPD Blue** star was no joke. He knew his Yankees baseball.

As if he needed to validate his fan card, Turturro's two young children, son Nick and daughter Apollonia, walked into the restaurant decked out in Yankees gear. When asked about their father's passion for his favorite team, they immediately began unleashing stories about the method behind their dad's madness.

Nick and Apollonia were well versed. It's obvious they had already followed their father's footsteps despite living on the West Coast. Forget the Dodgers. Forget the Angels. Those teams had no chance against the Yankees. Nick and Apollonia were already all about the pinstripes just like their fanatical father.

On Becoming a Fan
I became a Yankees fan in 1973. There was something about the original Yankee Stadium.

On the First Game He Attended
In '72, I went to a Mets game with a bunch of friends and I was afraid of heights. I freaked out. I didn't even enjoy the game. I thought I was going to blow off the mezzanine. My brother and my father liked boxing and basketball. Baseball I really discovered on my own. I went to a game with the Boy Scouts of America in '73, to the original Yankee Stadium, and the first time I walked in, I think it was in right field, with the blue seats, I was mesmerized. So I wound up going to a bunch of games. And just like that, I fell in love with the Yankees and Yankee Stadium.

On His Favorite Players
I loved Bobby Murcer, I loved Roy White, I loved [Thurman] Munson. I loved the way [Munson] ran the bases. I think after the game one day me and my friends hugged him. He had a beer in his hand, too. In this era, [Derek] Jeter, [Paul] O'Neill, and Tino [Martinez] were my guys. I really loved O'Neill.

On His Most Memorable Game
Probably the '76 Game 5 against the Royals in the ALCS. The Yankees led 6-3 until George Brett's homer to tie the game. Then [Chris] Chambliss hit a home run to right-center in the ninth to win the series. That was unbelievable.

The Conflicted Fan
Mike Francesa, Host of WFAN's "Mike'd Up"

Spending several decades as part of the sports media has changed the fan in Mike Francesa. In a way, he even considers that fandom a thing of the past. "Now, you wind up rooting for the people," the FAN's drive-time host explained. "It's all about the people and the relationships."

While that may be true, it's obvious during a brief conversation with the human baseball encyclopedia that his Yankees fandom is not completely stifled. He might believe that it no longer exists, but somewhere deeply imbedded in his subconscious, he's still an ardent supporter of the team—and not just certain players. All those years of rooting and idolizing Mickey Mantle don't fade so quickly from memory. That becomes evident when Mike starts pontificating about the Yankees' glorious past.

The dynamics, however, have changed a bit over the years. As a journalist, he views the games and results from a more professional point of view. But the bottom line is he still wants the Yankees to win. That never really changes. Just check the tapes. All those heated exchanges over the years with former partner Chris "Mad Dog" Russo—so many of them were over...the Yankees. That was not all business; there had to be more to it than that. Even when he's watching the game by himself, that same emotion is there for Mike. It was undeniably evident during the Yankees' 2009 World Series run.

On Becoming a Fan

[I grew up during] the time period when there was no other team in town. The Giants and Dodgers had left, and when I was a little boy, three or four years old, I had an older brother who was six years older, and he was a big Yankees fan. So I became a big Yankees fan, a big Mickey Mantle fan, at a very young age.... We were a Yankees household and that was basically it.

On His Favorite Player

Mantle was my only hero in my lifetime. I never had another hero. I had Mickey Mantle scrapbooks, watched every at-bat I could and everything else. I was a big Mickey Mantle fan.

On His Favorite Moments

Always Mantle. Mantle with his '64 World Series [game-winning] homer against Barney Schultz in Game 3, his 500th home run, his last couple of big games. He had a great run in '66 when he was healthy and before he got hurt. He had an incredible week when he went crazy. It was sort of like his last hurrah.

On His Favorite Players

Mantle, Bobby Murcer, and Bernie Williams, those were my three guys. All center fielders.

On the First Game He Attended

It was the summer of 1961 and Mantle, [Roger] Maris, and [Johnny] Blanchard hit home runs when they beat the Cleveland Indians. I thought every game was like that.

that the co-host of *Live with Regis and Kelly* is a big sports fan. Considering Regis was born and raised in the Bronx before attending Notre Dame, it only makes sense that he's a Yankees fan. Being pals with owner George Steinbrenner probably helps a little, too.

Keith Olbermann. He attended hundreds of Yankees games with his mother, who, before her death, attended something like 1,500 games herself, he estimates. How can you not be a die-hard Yankees fan with that kind of influence in your life? Even after years in the sports media, the well-known talk show host remains a regular at Yankee Stadium.

LeBron James. The great LeBron plays in Cleveland, was raised in nearby Akron, and has lived in the state of Ohio his entire life. Still, he's a Yankees fan—a real Yankees fan at that. When posed with the question of which team he roots for when the Indians play the Yankees, he didn't even blink. Yanks.

Jack Nicholson. "First of all, they wanted me to wear a Red Sox hat," he grumbled in a 2006 interview with *New York* magazine, speaking of his Boston-based character in *The Departed*. "But I said, all things being equal, I don't want to. My Yanks, they came before the Lakers, of course."

Artie Lange. Howard Stern's sidekick calls himself a "maniacal Yankees fan." If you listen to the show regularly, you know he's serious. He knows his stuff and supports his team.

The Mets

Jerry Seinfeld. "Jerry from Queens" always wants to talk Mets when he schmoozes with Steve Somers on the FAN. He considers the Mets' owners, the Wilpons, his "good friends" and has been a familiar face in the crowd at Shea and now Citi Field.

Glenn Close. The actress and Connecticut native is a well-known Mets fan. She's especially proud to have sung "God Bless America" at the very last game at Shea because she's "been going there many, many years."

Jon Stewart. You can tell he's a big Mets fan by the way he crushed Phillies fans on *The Daily Show* during a June 2009 episode. Or by the way the Mets happen to be a topic more than they should be on a national show. Ron Darling, Willie Randolph, and David Wright have all been featured as guests.

Matthew Broderick. The other half of the famous Mets-Yankees couple, Broderick has also held his ground nicely for his team. Broderick once said in an MSNBC interview, when speaking about the team's '07 collapse, "I don't really think we'll ever be over it. Now it's just part of the Mets experience, you know?" Spoken like a true die-hard.

Two true-blue (and orange) fans, Jerry Seinfeld and Matthew Broderick take in a game at the old Shea Stadium.

Julia Stiles. She wrote a piece about the opening of Citi Field in the *Wall Street Journal* which discussed the Mets bullpen and even dropped names like J.J. Putz and Daniel Murphy. She also reflected on the 2000 Subway Series as if it were yesterday. The wounds are still fresh, true signs that she's no phony.

Ray Romano. Like most fans of his generation, Ray got hooked on the '69 Mets. His not-so-loosely-autobiographical character on *Everybody Loves Raymond* is a dead giveaway. There's even an episode on which several of the '69 Mets make cameos.

Matt Dillon. He threw out the first pitch before the 2006 NLCS Game 6 between the Mets and the Cardinals. He also admittedly collects Mookie Wilson baseball cards. That says enough about his fandom for us.

Jim Breuer. You have to be a die-hard Mets fan if you can so eloquently explain how it feels. "They suck," the comic said in a radio interview when the team was floundering through the summer of '09. "It's like being in love with an alcoholic. It's like, you constantly defend her, and people are like, 'Dude, your alcoholic friend is a mess,' and you're like, 'Nah, you don't know her like I do.'"

The Knicks

Spike Lee. Let's give Spike credit for being there for so many Knicks games every season. He's the Knicks' Jack Nicholson, always there in the front row with a baggy jersey and fully into the action on the court. Lee even had some memorable tête-à-têtes with opposing players, most memorably Reggie Miller and Michael Jordan. Some fans even criticize him for giving opponents a little extra motivation. Regardless, Lee has been there through it all.

Woody Allen. Allen didn't become an ardent fan until the 1968–69 season, when the Knicks started to get really good. It was during that campaign that he started attending every game at Madison Square Garden with Diane Keaton. The legendary Howard Cosell actually secured him season tickets—seats that have gradually improved over the years. The accomplished director hasn't missed many games since.

Chris Rock. Rock is another committed season-ticket holder who can't stand to see his team lose. He likes the scrappers, the hardworking players who do the dirty work. David Lee was his favorite player on some of the Knicks' struggling teams. The comedian is also a die-hard Mets fan, so you know he's serious about his New York sports.

Calvin Klein. His most famous fan behavior was waltzing onto the court to speak with the Knicks' Latrell Sprewell during action in a 2003 game. The move prompted lawmakers to pass a "Calvin Klein Bill" that increased the fine levied against spectators who disrupt games.

Jerry Ferrara. The Brooklyn native and actor who portrays Turtle on *Entourage* is a self-proclaimed Knicks and Yankees die-hard. He maintains he knew the entire Yankees' roster at age five. The teams are also his go-tos whenever he takes to one of his other favorite hobbies: video games.

Tracy Morgan. The comedian and star on NBC's *30 Rock* considers himself "Blue, orange, and white for life" and calls Madison Square Garden a "special place" and the "center of the

Calvin Klein approaches Latrell Sprewell during a 2003 game. Not appropriate fan behavior, though we do acknowledge his enthusiasm.

Beyonce and Jay-Z are often on hand to add extra star-wattage to Nets games.

universe." Sounds like a die-hard Knicks fan to us, particularly since he labels Larry Johnson's four-point play as his best moment at the Garden.

The Nets

Jay-Z. Sure, there might be a little bias, as the legendary rapper is part owner of the team. Still, at least he is dedicated and willing to use his fame to better the fortunes of the team and recruit star players.

Beyonce Knowles. If Jay-Z was biased, then this one's off the charts. Still, in addition to lending her star power in the courtside seats, she has worked with the team directly, helping design some of the outfits for the Nets' dancers.

The Rangers

Tim Robbins. A regular at Madison Square Garden, not only was he there for Game 7 of the team's 1994 Stanley Cup triumph over Vancouver, but he actually drank champagne from the Cup that memorable night. The actor claims to own every highlight video ever released from that championship season—that's a

The Familial Fan
Boomer Esiason, Former NFL Quarterback and Current WFAN Morning Show Host

Believe it or not, Boomer Esiason's probably been to more professional hockey than football games, despite playing in the NFL for 14 years. The Long Island native started attending Rangers games with his father as a young child, and the tradition continues with him and his own children, Gunnar and Sydney.

Growing up, Boomer went to 10 to 12 games each year with his father. When he was quarterbacking the Cincinnati Bengals, he went to six or seven games during the NFL's off-season. Now that he's retired from football, he attends about 25 regular-season games with his kids and has been at every playoff game in the 21st century. That's a lot of Rangers games.

On Becoming a Fan

I was a young kid and my dad would take me to games at the Garden. For me, that was the thing I was most excited about. I would have my Rangers jersey on, my dad would come home from working in the city, and we'd get back on the Long Island Rail Road.

On Keeping the Tradition

When my son was born in 1991, I said that the first thing I was going to do was take him to a Rangers game. I did that before he was a year of age. He and I have since experienced every single one of the playoff games for the 1994 Cup run—to the point that they actually put us in their highlight film. I've been a longtime season-ticket holder. I'm doing with my son and my daughter what my father did with me. I'm doing with my kids what my father did with me. That is, create a bond through something that we all have a passion for. And that happens to be the blue jersey and Madison Square Garden.

On His Favorite Moment

Well, obviously for us, when they won the Stanley Cup [in '94].

His Most Memorable Game

It was Game 6 [of the Eastern Conference Finals] against the Devils. Mark Messier did not only guarantee the win, but he guaranteed it in the same city where the Devils play. It was on the back cover of all the newspapers on game day. I was thinking at the time, **This is going to be the kiss of death**…. I came to realize, after the game was over that night, that it was truly the best moment in professional sports history in the New York area because of all the pressure that came along with it.

die-hard move if we've ever seen one. Robbins is also equally dedicated to the Mets.

John McEnroe. Robbins wasn't the only one sipping from the Cup in '94. Tennis legend and Queens native McEnroe labeled Madison Square Garden "a frequent destination" where he watched his "beloved" Knicks and Rangers.

The Islanders

Christie Brinkley. "What you probably did not know is that I'm a hockey fan, and I love the New York Islanders." The cover girl, fitness and beauty expert, environmentalist, and mom said it herself in a 2007 Islanders commercial. And we'll believe anything that someone that good-looking says.

Kevin Connolly. It's no accident that Connolly's character in Entourage wears a lot of Islanders gear. The Long Island native is as big a fan as they come. "The Islanders are the pride and joy of Long Island," he said during one interview. "They're all we got out there."

Gary Dell'Abate. Even through their 21st-century struggles, "Baba Booey" has stuck with the Islanders. He's also a supporter of the Mets. And who can forget that infamous first pitch he "threw" in 2009? *The Howard Stern Show* producer is also a loyal Jets fan.

The Devils

Kevin Smith. He attends games, owns Devils gear (at the very least, a scarf), hates the competition, and sticks with his team

Proof positive that Jon Bon Jovi has been a fan of Big Blue since his hair metal days, the rocker poses here with Giants players Sean Landeta and Matt Bahr after the team's 1991 Super Bowl victory.

through thick and thin. His knowledge is so impressive he's even run a playoff blog on NHL.com for several years and frequently writes about hockey on his Twitter page. All signs point to the accomplished director and New Jersey native being a die-hard fan.

Joe Piscopo. "Mr. New Jersey" is also known as the ultimate Devils fan. The comedian's also an ardent Nets supporter. As he's explained: "These teams are like everything great about New Jersey: hardworking, not much recognition, winning."

Yogi Berra. His friendship with former owner John McMullen and his New Jersey roots drew the former Yankees great to the Devils. He was a regular in the owner's box at the old Brendan Byrne Arena. When McMullen sold the team, there was a stipulation in the deal that still gave the Hall of Famer special access to the team's training facility.

Shaquille O'Neal. A Newark native, he says he has "always been a Devils fan." We're not going to challenge him. Shaq is a big, scary man.

The Giants

Jon Bon Jovi. The acclaimed rocker is a football junkie who has even been called a psycho Giants fan. "I'm one of those guys who goes into mourning post–Super Bowl," he once said. Part owner of the now-defunct Arena Football League's Philadelphia Soul, Bon Jovi has been a tried and true supporter of Big Blue.

Andy Rooney. A longtime season-ticket holder, the *60 Minutes* commentator attends every home game. "Going to the Giants' home games is just something I do," he said. You can't question his fandom when he admits to watching approximately 10 hours of football each weekend.

Sean "Diddy" Combs. "I'm an overall New York Giants fan," he said in an interview before the Giants' Super Bowl XXLII triumph.

Jordin Sparks. The *American Idol* winner sang the national anthem at the 2008 Super Bowl. Oh, and her father, Phillippi, played cornerback for the team, too.

The True "Blue" Fan
Joe Gannascolli, Actor

For the better part of four decades, Joe Gannascolli's been there with the Giants. The *Sopranos* actor has never abandoned them. "True Giants fans don't do that," he wrote in a *Daily News* guest column before Super Bowl XXLII.

Consider the Giants' shocking Super Bowl XXLII run as an example. Early in the regular season, Gannascolli had a group of five or six fans over who watched the games together. That grew to 15 or 16 late in the year, to 40 during the first playoff game in Dallas, 50 or 60 for the NFC Championship Game against Green Bay, and finally to around 100 for the Super Bowl. Oh, and he even dyed his dog blue for that Super Bowl. Now **that's** a die-hard fan.

On Becoming a Fan
It dates back to 1971. I was a Yankees fan, and it was only natural to become a Giants fan too.

On the Ultimate Sign of Fandom
I painted the lawn with the Giants logo and some players' numbers during the ['08] playoff run. I also kept putting the opposing quarterback's numbers with a slash through them. For the Super Bowl, I had an effigy of Tom Brady hanging in front of my house.

The Jets

Kevin James. The actor and comedian has been a Jets fan since the team's Shea Stadium days. His dad was a fan, and he followed. He even named his daughter Shea. As if we need more convincing, he's promised to drop whatever he is doing and be there if the Jets ever make the Super Bowl.

Adam Sandler. Despite spending most of his childhood in New England after being born in Brooklyn, he stuck with the same team that his father loved. The proof is also in his movies. In *Big Daddy*, the little boy wanted "the goddamn Jets" to win; in *Mr. Deeds*, he was informed that he owned the team; Dan Marino couldn't sell his soul for a Super Bowl in *Little Nicky* because Satan was a Jets fan.

Chris Berman. The ESPN sportscaster is a former season-ticket holder who idolized Joe Namath. "Boomer" was there back in the Shea days and still keeps an eye on the team.

Mike Greenberg. Another ESPN personality who has Jets ties, Greeny isn't shy about it. His love for former Jets QB Chad Pennington has been well documented over the years, as has his special affection for the team.

Larry David. The creator of *Seinfeld* and *Curb Your Enthusiasm* is so dedicated and knowledgeable that the former Jets coach Eric Mangini went to the fan for advice back in 2007. Amazingly, that isn't a joke.

Hayden Panettiere. The *Heroes* star declared on a Super Bowl pregame show that she was a Jets booster. We gladly accept her, regardless of her fan credentials.

CHECKLIST

THE TEST OF FANDOM

How big a fan are you? Are you a real fan? Let's find out. Answer each question with a Yes or No and tally the total at the end.

1. Do you have only one favorite team in each sport?

2. Do you own at least one piece of paraphernalia for each of your favorite teams?

3. Do you plan your schedule around sporting events?

4. Do you attend at least one game each season?

5. Do you watch or listen to a large majority of your team's games?

6. Do you know the entire roster of your favorite team?

7. Have you ever cried tears of joy for your team?

8. Have you ever attended a road game outside the Tri-State area featuring one of your teams?

9. Have you ever broken something out of anger after a loss or bad play?

10. Have you ever wished bodily harm on a player?

11. Do you know the uniform number of every player on your favorite team?

12. Do you have a room dedicated exclusively to your favorite team?

13. Have you ever attended every home game in a single season?

14. As an adult, have you ever written a letter to the team, owner, player, or front office?

15. Have you ever turned down sex because of a game?

16. Since adulthood, have you ever (literally) cried over a loss by your team?

17. Have you ever driven more than 10 hours to see a game?

18. Have you ever watched every game, every minute, every second, every pitch of an entire season for any of your favorite teams?

19. Have you snuck a peek at your team's score or highlight during sex?

20. Have you ever refused to date someone or ended a relationship based on their sports allegiance?

Scoring

Each yes on questions 1–5 is worth 1 point each

Each yes on questions 6–10 is worth 3 points each

Each yes on questions 11–15 is worth 4 points each

Each yes on questions 16–20 is worth 12 points each

If you scored 0 points: Don't even bother talking about sports. Ever.

If you scored 1–5 points: You're a *phony fan*. From the outside, you might appear to be a real fan because you adhere to some of the rules and know what you're talking about. Really, though, you're little more than a hollow shell with questionable dedication.

If you scored 6–20 points: You're a *solid fan*. You know what you're talking about and are willing to make small sacrifices to satisfy your fandom. But you're not willing to take that extra step to go over the top.

If you scored 21–40 points: You're a true *die-hard*. You possess the knowledge, dedication, and desire to consider yourself a real New York sports fan.

If you scored 41–80 points: You're pretty sick, but you're for sure a *real fan*. Not many things are more important to you than your team or, more likely, teams. They are pretty much on par with your spouse or love interest. Marriage counseling or psychological help could be necessary.

If you scored 81–100 points: You're *past the point of no return*. Get a life. If nothing else is as important as your rooting interests, you need help.